Flow

Keeping Your Heart Alive When Life Hurts

Joy Scott

A Word About Flow

After engaging with this book, I believe anyone who struggles with the whys and injustices that seem to infiltrate our lives as beloved children of God will be able to understand that there is freedom and joy on the other side.

Joy helps us understand grace and provides practical steps that lead to the need for maturity in embracing God's character and nature in a fallen world.

It's a love story that leads us to the profound truth that our faith is not based on what we think God should or shouldn't do, what He will or will not do, but upon our love relationship with Him.

Reading *Flow* will settle any heart that struggles with the toughest of times, life's traumas, and what seems to be outrageous injustices.

This book is well-written and immerses me as a reader with truth, practicality, and power. It is a must-read for those who truly desire to know the freedom and joy that is always available...as we trust Him.

I had the privilege of pastoring Joy when she was a young teenager in our youth group, and I have enjoyed watching her bloom into the woman of faith she is today. Her book is the most authentic expression of what true religion is: Loving Jesus and others - no matter what life throws your way.

I see Jesus in her today as I always have.

Pastor Kathy Pedeaux | The Mission Church

M.S. Counseling/Psychology

Executive Director | Riverbend Counseling

Brave one — You've endured much.

Still, you contend for your heart. This book is dedicated to you.

IMPACT61
collective

Impact61 Collective, LLC

This title may be purchased in bulk for educational, business, fund raising, or sales promotional use. For information, please email jonjoyscott@gmail.com..

Unless otherwise noted, Scripture quotations are taken from the ESV© Bible (The Holy Bible, English Standard Version*), copyright © 2001 by Crossway, a publishing ministry of Good News Publishers. Used by permission. All rights reserved.

Scripture quotations marked NIV are taken from the Holy Bible, New International Version', NIV', Copyright © 1973, 1978, 1934, 2011 by Biblica, Inc. Used by permission of Zondervan, All rights reserved worldwide. www.zondervan.com. The "NIV" and "New International Version" are trademarks registered in the United States Patent and Trademark Office by Biblica, Inc."

Scripture quotations marked CEV are taken from the Contemporary English Version. Copyright © 1991, 1992, 1995 by American Bible Society. Used by permission.

Scripture quotations marked NKJV are taken from the New King James Version*, © 1982 by Thomas Nelson. Used by permission. All rights reserved.

Scripture quotations marked NLT are taken from the Holy Bible, New Living Translation. © 1996, 2004, 2007, 2013 by Tyndale House Foundation. Used by permission of Tyndale House Publishers, Inc., Carol Stream, Illinois 60188, All rights reserved.

Scripture quotations marked NASB are taken from the New American Standard Bible® (NASB), © 1960, 1962, 1963, 1968, 1971, 1972, 1973, 1975, 1977, 1995, 2020 by The Lockman Foundation.Used by permission. All rights reserved.

Book design by Sarah Geringer

Paperback ISBN: 979-8-9997511-0-2

eBook ISBN: 979-8-9997511-1-9

Printed in the United States of America

Contents

How to Use This Book

This book was written with your healing, growth, and spiritual journey in mind. Whether you're reading it on your own or walking through it with others, you'll find encouragement, truth, and tools to help you move from pain to purpose, and from stuck places into the *FLOW* of God's grace.

You can read this book personally, journaling through the questions at your own pace, or with a small group, meeting together over 8 meetings. Let the stories, principles, and Scripture breathe life into your heart. Pause often. Let God speak. Don't rush the process - healing and transformation will unfold.

If you're using this resource in a small group, I've designed a simple flow to help you experience the most impact together:

- Before your first group meeting, everyone should read Chapters 1-4. These chapters lay the foundation and prepare each heart for the journey ahead.

- Over the following weeks, group members can read Chapters 5-10 individually, reflecting on the questions and applying the principles personally.

- Chapters 11-12 are best read together, bringing your stories, insights, and progress into a shared space of encouragement and breakthrough.

Discussion questions can be used for personal reflection or powerful group conversation and are found in the back of the book. These questions are designed to go deeper—into your heart, your walk with God, and connection with others.

My prayer is that this book doesn't just inform you — *it transforms you*. Whether you're walking through disappointment, trauma, or just hungry for more, this journey is for you. And remember, you're not alone. Let God guide every step—and if you're walking with others, lean in and cheer each other on.

You're about to step into something beautiful. Let's go!

Flow

An Introduction

Pain, depression, and resentment gripped me to my core. It did not happen overnight. About a decade and a half of culminating events reached a tipping point. Standing at a crossroads, I did not know what to do - and doing nothing was still a choice. All the pain and anger were jumbled inside of me. I asked myself repeatedly, "What do I do now? How do I dig my way out of years of compounded, unresolved pain and trauma?" I wanted it all to go away, yet I didn't know how to get it away from me.

The resentment I nursed seemed justifiable. The multiple circumstances outside of my control brought uninvited pain that felt impossible to sort. I was in the center of the sinking quicksand. How did I end up here? I had to make a critical choice. I vividly remember the morning I stood outside my front door and lost the strength to go on. A defining moment presented itself. The next choice I made would determine my future. Unable to bear my concealed pain, I knew what was at stake—my destiny and purpose.

I then heard the gentle, inner voice of the Holy Spirit whisper to me, *"Joy, if you don't reach out and trust again, you are not going to make it."* I knew what this meant. I was not going to fulfill my purpose. I was either going to live stuck, bitter, addicted to some form of coping mechanism, or even worse—yield to the temptation to end my life. How did I know Jesus all my life, yet find myself in such a broken place?

After sorting through fear, panic, and pride, I bravely picked up the phone. I called the person I knew I was supposed to call with a disclaimer up front, "I cannot afford for you to misunderstand or mishandle me." I courageously told her exactly where I was. She heard me. She understood me. She nurtured me. I felt a release. I had held the pain alone for so long, but no more.

That bold step began the journey of my clogged-up heart beginning to *FLOW* again. This step led to another step, then another in releasing the blockages hindering me.

If you live long enough, we all will eventually have an unwelcome confrontation with pain. The crossing could happen early in life, or wait to approach later, but one thing is certain: this intruder will come. When it comes, those who know how to navigate and pivot the roadblocks it throws will process through it with a renewed perspective and purpose.

You may be reading this book because you have experienced the unthinkable. Maybe you have not experienced a life-shattering event, but you carry a disguised subtle pain that lurks and lingers making cynicism and negativity its home. Perhaps it is the prolonged disappointment of being overlooked year after year, or a deep resentment that crept in and is slowly paralyzing your heart. It could be the subtle pain of an untrue voice you made an agreement with that is stealing your joy.

Oftentimes, the subtlety of pain blockages can cause you to remain stuck in your heart and not even realize it.

This book is for all of you—those who have experienced deep trauma and pain and those of you who have experienced the subtle, ongoing pain of simply living on this earth.

I understand this kind of pain when wave after wave of circumstances add to the previous hits. Before you know it, you are internally stuck with negative thoughts and emotions circulating and a cloud of heaviness trying to claim your daily life. When you experience such loss and pain, you can begin to question if God is really good. If He is good, why did He allow the losses you have encountered? I've wrestled with these questions when the unthinkable crossed my life as well. My prayer is to help answer some of your questions by unveiling my life to you and by bringing you to the Bible as the most reliable source of answers.

I have literally fought for my life, my heart, and my destiny in God. The *FLOW* I am experiencing in my life now is due to the healing and revelation I am going to share with you in this book. That critical crossroad and my "Yes" to keep my heart alive brought me back to life.

Proverbs 4:23 says, *"Keep your heart with all vigilance, for from it flow the springs of life."* With this verse as our premise, we find a clear path to process our pain in Psalm 139.

This psalm reveals a biblical guide to unlock our hearts when we become paralyzed by painful life circumstances. Together, we will learn how to "keep our hearts" and "flow the springs of life." We will learn where the true source of pain comes from in this life and how to get unstuck from its torment.

You and I were created to *FLOW* in hope, overcome the schemes against us, and live this life knowing we are lavishly loved. We were not created for pain, but for peace and purpose!

By sharing my story and also the stories of other courageous women, I pray you unearth everything God desires for you. Will you take this brave step with me as we courageously examine our hearts together and unleash the stuck places?

Grab some friends to join you on this journey. We need each other's support, interdependency, and vulnerability to *FLOW!* Buckle up!

Chapter 1

Divorced. Disqualified. Devastated...But Not Done.

"...Bind up the broken-hearted and set the captives free."

Isaiah 61:1

When I sensed a call to surrender my life to ministry at age 18, I could not fathom it would be from the depth of my own brokenness and pain I have overcome today. At this young age, I knew Isaiah 61 was my calling, but was not pre-pared for how this would unfold in my life. Isaiah 61:1 says, *"I have called you to bind up the broken hearted and set the cap-tives free. To comfort all who mourn."* These verses were inspiring. I thought, "Sign me up and let's go!" I was passionate and loved God as a young teenager.

Little did I know then, I would walk through many years of my own heartache before I helped to see anyone set-free or comforted anyone with a broken heart. Back then I thought I had all the answers, like many young zealots do, as I preached boldly to encourage others in schools and campuses around my hometown.

When I was in high school and college, I did not date just any guy; I was praying for the right one. I knew there was a unique path for me and I was not going to "settle" for anyone less than who was right for me. At 14, I can remember being so in love with Jesus and passionate about His plan for me. I wanted to give my whole life to Him. I carried a purity of heart and a sensitive ear to the things of God, but had an underdeveloped identity and confidence.

Being well-liked in high school, I was voted homecoming queen and the "Miss" of the Mr. and Miss titles voted by my high school peers my senior year. I was the captain of my sports teams and voted as a leader in the clubs I was involved in. As I entered college, I continued with this passion for God and being admired by my peers. I won the title of "Miss Southeastern Louisiana University" and was actively involved in ministry life on my campus. I was eager to give my all to God.

After graduating college and beginning a teaching career, I knew I was called to serve in full-time ministry in a unique way, but not in a traditional church setting. I decided to go to Youth With a Mission discipleship training school for five months. Just before I left for Texas, I met someone who seemed just as passionate as I was about following God. We started dating, then I left for five months.

We dated long-distance for five months and before I came home from this school, we decided we wanted to get married. Right before I came home, we got into an over-the-phone conflict that left me crushed. He seemed unempathetic and I should have noticed the red flags, but we were too far down the road.

I chose to ignore those red flags because I was getting older and desired to be married. All my friends were getting married and it was the next logical step in life. Walking down the aisle, I was a spotless young bride bursting with dreams for an amazing future, but those dreams soon shriveled to nothing.

In just a few short months those joyful expectations metamorphosed into sorrow. I walked down the aisle and all the colors of my beautiful, brilliant life turned to splatters of black and gray. My bright future of helping others seemed over. I could not even help myself. The intense pain left me with no craving for food. My body withered away to mere skin and bones.

Unbelievably, I found myself imprisoned in a diabolical, controlling marriage. Not many months into the marriage, my husband began punishing me. If I did anything to displease him, such as not asking permission before purchasing something or wearing clothes he did not approve, I was then manipulated and punished. At times, for my own "inappropriate" behavior, I was told to write out Scripture verses over and over to correct my pathetic behavior.

In countless ways, I was told I was, "Ugly, ugly, ugly!" These words rolled around in my mind constantly. During that time I thought they must be true if my own husband thinks so.

My young husband told me I would never be fully loved by him because I was "unattractive." I forgot I was the homecoming queen and Miss Southeastern Louisiana University.

I forgot how admired and lovable I was by so many others and I allowed this one voice to dictate.

Time and again, I was told I was like the biblical character, Leah - ugly and unloved. In the Bible book of Genesis, the story recounted Abraham's grandson, Jacob. Jacob was madly in love with beautiful Rachel. Jacob worked for her hand in marriage for seven years. At the end of the seven years, Jacob was deceived by his father-in-law and was tricked into marrying her sister, Leah. Rachel was beautiful and loved, while her sister, Leah, was not. My young husband was convinced that he was Jacob and I was his Leah. He felt there was a "Rachel" out there that would make him happy - yet he was stuck with me, his "Leah." He would daily pick out my clothes to help me become "more attractive" - although those clothes looked unattractive and homely.

In the Genesis account, Jacob really did not love Leah, but she endured to the end. I was encouraged to do the same. Insanely, he tried to encourage me that I was actually blessed, "because Leah was in the direct lineage of Jesus." Clearly, I was in an ugly, abusive, demented relationship. But there was one thing I vowed I would never do - get divorced. I was raised once you say, "I do," you *did*. I went from a confident, fun-loving beauty queen to a controlled shell of a soul.

In my fear of divorce and the labels that ensued, I was determined I was going to pray, get counseling, and patiently endure the piercing pain until God broke through to him, "like a good, godly wife should."

For two years, I rode the carousel of waking up and going to bed crying out of crippling pain and rejection. Looking into the mirror all I could see was "Ugly, ugly, ugly!' Slowly, I began to believe the lies I was being told and began to despise my physical body. I saw myself through a lens that was projected onto me. Daily, I was tormented and compared myself to other girls thinking, *"She's Rachel. She has what it takes to make him happy."* I lived deeply tormented in my soul, believing I was not enough.

Deep down I knew how precious I was to God, but it was all I could do to withstand the avalanche of destructive words and abuses showering me. All of the times I was told by God in prayer that I was beautiful and uniquely made began to secure my true identity. I had to break agreement with the oppression I was facing.

After much counseling and prayer, it became clear I had some tough decisions to make if I was going to heal. Would I place my expectations on my abusive husband or look to my Heavenly Father to protect and restore me? The choice was mine to make. I asked God all of the questions as to how I ended up in this relationship. Was I blind? Was it my fault? Was I stubborn and ignorant of negative clues?

Devastated, I now had the label "divorced" written over me. It felt like I was labeled these words:

"Divorced, Disqualified, Disappointed."

All my dreams shattered. When my life's dreams were demolished into a billion pieces beyond recognition, God showed me who I really was. I was his beloved, beautiful, bold daughter. I was adorable to him. I made his heart smile. I was a broken woman with a sincere relationship with Jesus. It was the love of God that loved me back to life. I was literally loved back to life.

There is a love found in God that is overwhelmingly more than enough. I pray, dear friend, you know this kind of love in your life, no matter what you have been told or experienced.

Several years later, my current husband, Jon, was miraculously placed into my life. He was and still is God's gift of redemption to me. Jon spoke words of life over me and his actions proved how lovable I am, which restored that previous awful season of my life.

We did not know what the future held, but until then, we had two baby boys 14 months apart within the first three years of marriage. Life was all-consuming, fun, and full of surprises; then we were slapped with a big surprise. One month before our oldest son, Joseph, turned four years old, we discovered a large stage four tumor on his brainstem.

I can remember the moment the doctor came in with tearful eyes to tell us. I collapsed into the arms of my Heavenly Father again. He had held me before. I was familiar with His loving embrace. I heard the gentle whisper, *"You are not alone. I am holding you, Joy."* For the following five months we fought with everything in us until we watched our firstborn son take his last breath.

I know what it is like to desire to yield to the temptation to become bitter, find a coping mechanism, and just get by. I know the temptation to just grow hard of heart.

I thought I already went through the worst pain a person could bear, but now this. My firstborn son. Cancer. How does a child get cancer? Surely, God could have stopped this - right? I was angry with God. He is the one who told me I was not alone.

He was holding me. He already knew this was going to happen. *Why did this have to happen?*

As if this was not enough for a lifetime of pain, there were many more circumstances I will share in the chapters ahead which led to a severe, two-year depression. When we carry around accumulated, unprocessed pain, we reach a limit. We shut down. We are stuck and it manifests in depression.

I have experienced enough to know that even when we do everything "right," painful experiences can still happen. It is how we process those painful circumstances that will determine if we will move on to overcoming or not. It is what we believe about those painful circumstances that will determine our future. The temptation is at its peak when we are in intense pain to partner with a lie from hell.

My friend, we were not created to be beat-up all throughout life, but I know first-hand we live in a fallen-world. Bad things happen. People make dumb choices. We have a real enemy who wants to take us out. We also have a *bigger* God who has given us the ability to have an abundant life - no matter our painful circumstances.

I want to demonstrate to you, not by my mere words, but by my example. I want to teach you how to tend your heart when it feels shattered into a million pieces. I want to show you how God can transform every pain into something beautiful. He can transform any circumstance and turn it into a master-piece. Only He can do it! I would love to know your story one day, but today I am going to share mine.

I am also going to tell you how to go from stuck to unstuck. It's not a quick fix, but it works if we embrace the steps. Here I am, all these years later, living out Isaiah 61:1 after all - *"To bind up the broken-hearted and set the captives free."*

Our bodies are masterfully designed to *FLOW*. The synchrony and systems of our brilliantly orchestrated body gives us life. When the movement of this creative design is restrained, we begin to deteriorate.

In the same way, the Creator designed our hearts to *FLOW* to support physical life. He also intended for our inner heart to *FLOW* to uphold emotional and spiritual health. The vitality of body, soul, and spirit determine our ability to fulfill our God-given purposes.

Just as we care for our physical hearts, we also must care for our inner hearts to thrive. Our body, soul, and spirit are integrated and influence momentum in life. When one area is injured, it impairs the other areas. As we cultivate health in all three areas, we can remain resilient against the destructive schemes of the enemy who tries to inject pain, shame, and rejection into our souls, just like he did to mine. In his dark mind, the earlier he can do this in your life, the better. We can learn to become wise and overcome these ploys that try to derail us and our loved ones from our God-given authority and destiny.

The wise king Solomon said, *"Keep your heart with all vigilance, for from it* **FLOW** *the springs of life."* (Proverbs 4:23, emphasis mine.) This verse does not speak about our physical heart, but the inner heart: a supple, inner world of the soul that has bounce. This is a bounce that absorbs negative circumstances and still rises up to give something positive back. A buoyant heart rebounds when stones are thrown and arrows scheme to pierce. The tending of a healthy soul is what Proverbs 4:23 unveils, and it is also my heart's desire for you.

Have you ever seen someone get hurt, betrayed, or disappointed and then watched as their heart began to shrivel? Has this ever happened to you? When your heart shrinks, the "springs of life" can't properly *FLOW*. "Springs of life" can be interpreted as alive, raw, fresh, and strong. The strength and vitality of your soul become restricted when the "springs of life" are hindered. As a result, you cannot function as you have been divinely designed.

Conversely, have you ever seen someone with weathered, wrinkly skin beam with positivity, encouragement, and blessing toward others? I know older people who have endured the unthinkable and are still hearty of soul. What is the difference between a person who locks up and one who flows out?

Ultimately, I have discovered when life is painful, we have two options:

1. To shrivel in heart, stay, and be limited. (Passive Posture)

2. To "keep" (guard and filter) our hearts to protect the *FLOW*. (Active Posture)

How do you tend your heart in such a way that it remains vibrant when life gets *really* hard? How can the Holy Spirit *FLOW* through you for His purposes - despite your fragile human container? How can you steward your heart and soul to finish your race with strength and love on the inside?

By the grace of God, my hope, prayer, and desire is to clarify these questions by helping you explore the deep crevices of your heart while applying Scripture, bringing awareness, and receiving love as a guide. You can unleash your heart to FLOW again, even when life is painful.

I have faced crossroads with difficult choices to make more than I would have preferred. My heart, on many occasions, was obliterated. It felt natural to just wither and find coping mechanisms to survive.

I know what it feels like not to want to live another day due to pain too much to bear. I have endured extreme abuse, a devastating divorce, the death of a child, and delayed dreams, disappointments, and betrayal. Together, I want to help you process your pain so you can FLOW again, just as I have fought and learned to do by His grace.

In the coming chapters, I will share my story and those of other inspiring women I know who have persevered in heart and are continuing to FLOW.

I want to offer you this hope right now. If you are in pain or your heart has withered, get ready to open those dams, which wait to be unleashed, and allow the loving work of the Holy Spirit to heal you. Learning how to tend our hearts is a skill we, as children of God, must be proficient in so we can be strong, radiant, and wise to our enemy's traps.

Our flowing hearts are connected to our relationships. Our relationships are connected to our purpose. Our purpose is connected to the corporate purpose of the Body of Christ and, ultimately, God's Kingdom on the earth and in eternity.

Chapter 2

Kinked, But Why?

When your reactions to life don't make sense

I was born and raised in southern Louisiana's heat, humidity, and hurricanes. Natives of South Louisiana are keenly aware of the weather conditions that can abruptly rise over the surrounding waters from June to September. We enjoy our summers, but in the back of Louisianian minds, we are all thinking the same thing: *"Will we have a major hurricane this year?"* Some of you face earthquakes, tornadoes, or even tsunamis, but we contend with the unpredictability of abrupt hurricanes.

A few summers ago, after a mild hurricane passed through, I was out cleaning the yard with our two boys. My husband was back to work, and there was much to be done to get our yard in order. We live in a neighborhood with many mature trees. While there are pros to having gorgeous trees in the yard, hurricanes passing through is a con. I grew up in the country on 40 acres, so I love some sweat and outside work. That day, I was on a roll and could not stop. My yard pile was growing like a teenager on summer break. I had fulfilling momentum, so I thought, "I'll just burn this pile and keep going."

My boys were happy to strike the match and light it up. (What is it with boys and fire anyway?) Up it went! The extra pine straw we threw in was the fuel to a full-grown fire at record speed. I looked up and thought,

"Fire Department!"

I was not expecting the flames to be quite so enormous. The colossal blaze was close to catching a nearby tree on fire. My youngest son scrolled to find the fire department's number and was ready to dial. I yelled at my older son to turn on the hose and sprint it over. He speedily delivered the solution. I squeezed the nozzle for water and...

NOTHING!

Nothing came out!

When I needed water in a crucial time, it was not there. The water was turned on. It was coming out of the pipe, BUT... the hose had a KINK! Yes, "kink" - that's what we call it in the country. I can still hear my niece say, "Paw Paw, the hose has a 'kank' in it!" ("Kank" is the extra-country version of kink.)

The kinked hose was rolled up in a storage container, so I did not have time to figure out where the blockage was coming from. Thankfully, we had another hose on the other side of the house, so I called for that one. The secondary hose worked properly, and I brought the flames down without setting the neighborhood ablaze or embarrassingly calling the fire department. My adrenaline subsided. We unanimously agreed that all yard work was done for the day.

Many times, we can be like the kinked hose. The hose was made to carry water from one place to another. It was designed for simple human purposes, like putting out fires or watering gardens. When the water flows, the hose does what it is manufactured to do. When it is kinked, we must stop to fix the problem. We cannot move on with our tasks until we unravel the kink.

Sometimes, our hearts fail to flow, like a kinked hose. Our physical heart can have blockage, but I am speaking of our inner heart - our mind, will, and emotions. Matthew 5:8 says, *"Blessed are the pure in heart, for they will see God."*

How do you have a pure or "unkinked" heart? How do you cultivate a heart that can *FLOW* and function with the design of the Creator? How can you nurture a heart ready to *FLOW*, as opposed to a heart stuck, stifled, and stagnant? A stagnant or "kinked" heart cannot flow in the way it was designed. When life needs your heart to be open, the blockage can hinder a healthy path forward.

My friend, Emma, had her fair share of barriers at an early age. She was 13 when her parents divorced. As a child, she was misunderstood and mishandled. She spent too much time alone, while her parents were busy with themselves to attend to her needs. To no one's surprise, she clung to her abusive boyfriend and became pregnant at age 14. Loved ones encouraged Emma to have an abortion, even though it was not what she wanted.

Right before pursuing what she was convinced as the only option, a woman implanted the idea of another way. Emma did not go through with the abortion. She ended up living in a girls' home and choosing to be a birth mother.

She gave birth to a beautiful baby boy and did the bravest thing: she gave her son to another family to raise. Emma tried to carry on with her life after this traumatic event, but was experiencing kinks. She was unaware of her trauma, unprocessed pain, and undefined identity. She knew she reacted in extreme ways and had a severe undertow of anxiety driving her decisions while others seemed calm. She did not understand why she went from 0 to 10 in a nanosecond. She assumed she was just extra high strung.

Fast-forward about 20 years, and that's when my path collided with Emma's. I met Emma at a church retreat. The retreat was designed to help people find freedom from oppressive bondages affecting their lives. Some of the topics were guilt, shame, pride, and sexual bondages. I was serving as a prayer minister at the end of each session. Emma's friend was next in line for me to pray for her at the end of one session. Instead of stepping forward to me, she pushed Emma in front of her and said, "She needs to pray for you." It was a divine appointment!

We had a powerful prayer time and Emma experienced profound freedom and joy. Since that retreat, we have become beautiful warrior friends. We have been in the trenches together in countless hard times. We had a powerful prayer time and Emma experienced profound freedom and joy. Emma has decided to pursue freedom in every part of her life. After the retreat, Emma began reclaiming her spiritual freedom. She wanted more of what God had for her and her family. I have never seen someone more determined to receive healing in her life and family. She wanted it for her heart, spirit, mind, will, and emotions. Emma now shares her story with others. She does this as she works to *FLOW* in her life instead of giving in to less than who God has created her to be.

Emma spent many years restricted. Then she discovered she needed freedom to *FLOW*. She was "kinked" and didn't know it. She had an inaccurate view of herself and, thus, lived limited and less than what Jesus died to give her.

Once Emma met Christ, she could reject her old limitations and receive God's truth in her life. Once she found her true identity in Christ, she could reject false beliefs she partnered with suggested by the enemy from pain, trauma, and abuse and receive all Jesus had for her. She is having more and more freedom and has shattered the enemy's grip in her life.

"Therefore, if anyone is in Christ, he is a new creation. The old has passed away; behold, the new has come." 2 Corinthians 5:17

Because Emma was "kinked," she lived her life protecting herself from the next disappointment she was accustomed to experiencing. Protecting herself was her posture, even when there was no danger. She had been through so much trauma. The trauma was so deeply embedded inside her body, she did all she could to survive. Survival mode is an automatic reaction when we have traveled through such pain. We self-protect, control, and keep walls up until we feel safe enough to loosen our grip. It takes a brave person like Emma to pursue healing and learn how to *FLOW* again. It is possible!

Maybe you have had circumstances like Emma's. Perhaps you experienced something different. Pain is still pain. Trauma is still trauma. Loss is still loss. Stuck is still stuck.

Like Emma, I also have experienced severe pain, loss, and trauma. I have endured abuse, rejection, divorce, the death of a child to cancer, and prolonged pain in my soul that shut me down with depression. I also have experienced a *FLOW* of freedom, love, purpose, and joy from walking with the Holy Spirit.

Have you, like Emma and me, been "kinked" and didn't even know it? Are you "kanked?" (Ha!) Are you living in a way that reacts to painful past experiences? We can survive an entire lifetime with a reaction to pain and trauma without even realizing it. But we don't have to do this. My desire is to encourage you to receive healing and live a *FLOW*ing, joyful, and purpose-filled life.

Trauma does not have to end in tragedy!

I would like to ask you this question: "What is the condition of your heart?" Maybe there is a blockage hindering your *FLOW*. Perhaps it is subtle or maybe it's substantial. What is happening underneath the surface of your heart which requires attention? Are you carrying pain? Have you been hurt to the point it drains your mind and energy? What situations in life or relationships leave you feeling disappointed?

How is unforgiveness or bitterness haunting you? Do you look at people through a skeptical lens? Are you afraid the rug will be pulled out from underneath you when times are good? I want you to be brutally honest with yourself, and remember, this is between you and God. I am stopping now to pray for every one of you as you courageously and bravely ask the loving Father to examine your heart.

I want to invite you to take some time to answer the questions below. Read through each one and ask the Holy Spirit to reveal anything hidden. Allow Him to search your heart.

"Search me, God, and know my heart; test me and know my anxious thoughts. See if there is any offensive way in me, and lead me in the way everlasting." Psalm 139:23-24 (NIV)

You are completely known by the Father, the Son (Jesus), and the Holy Spirit—the Trinity—three in One. You need each role of our God to lean on. He will reveal Himself in every way to you. He doesn't reveal to condemn you. He reveals to love and heal you. It takes courage to open your eyes to see the truth of where you are.

"Then you will know the truth, and the truth will set you free." John 8:32 (NIV)

Answer the questions below to see if you may be "kinked" and not know it. Ask the Holy Spirit to show you. Don't be afraid. Without acknowledging the truth, we can't be free. We will get the kinks out together throughout the rest of this book! Just like my friend Emma, you can be brave, take an honest look, and find freedom. You are not alone! Prayerfully and honestly answer the questions below as you search your heart. You can journal your answers on the pages here.

How do you try to control situations to avoid discomfort? Do you do this instead of honestly sharing your insecurities?

_____

_____

_____

How do you approach your relationships when you feel insecure? Avoid? Hide? Anger? Attack? Medicate? Ignore? Numb?

_____

_____

_____

What triggers you in certain scenarios?

_____

_____

_____

What opportunities do you avoid out of the fear of failure?

_____

_____

_____

How do you accept a lower standard so you are not rejected?

_____

_____

_____

How do you control your loved ones, children, and situations to make yourself feel less vulnerable?

_____

_____

_____

What irrational fears paralyze you?

_____

_____

_____

How do you shy away from letting people fully know you out of fear you are not enough or to avoid rejection?

_____

_____

_____

What negative thoughts bombard your mind regularly?

_____

_____

_____

How do you hide the real you to be acceptable to others?

_____

_____

_____

After honestly answering the previous questions, could you use some "spring cleaning" of the heart? One thing I know for sure is that you can FLOW with joy and peace again or for the very first time.

Congratulations on taking this brave step! You did it by taking an honest look at your heart! You are amazing and loved, my friend!

What is God speaking to you? Write what He is revealing to you now. Take your time, and I'll see you in Chapter 3 when you are ready.

Chapter 3

Heart Stoppers

The world is bleeding from a silent epidemic—trauma. It's clogging the heart, stopping where love and purpose were meant to flow.

      I understand what it is like to have the imprint of trauma on my life. Trauma's imprint can also be seen in our nation and around the world. On a typical day, there are more than 20,000 phone calls placed to domestic violence hotlines nationwide, according to the National Coalition Against Domestic Violence.[1] Twelve million people per year are physically abused by an intimate partner, and 29 percent of women in the United States have been raped.[2] This is merely physical trauma, not to mention the emotional trauma which exists. When the imprint of trauma marks a person's life, the ability to *FLOW* from a healthy heart is blocked.

What exactly is trauma anyway? I am not an expert in understanding trauma, so I will only quote those who are. Trauma is when we experience very stressful, frightening, or distressing events that are difficult to cope with or out of our control. Another explanation says that it results from exposure to an incident or series of events that are emotionally disturbing or life-threatening with lasting adverse effects on the individual's functioning and mental, physical, social, emotional, and spiritual well-being. Some examples of trauma include: an accident, crime, natural disaster, physical or emotional abuse, neglect, experiencing or witnessing violence, death of a loved one, war, and more.

Bessel van der Kolk MD, author of *"The Body Keeps the Score,"* reports, "Research by the Centers for Disease Control and Prevention has shown that one in five Americans was sexually molested as a child; one in four was beaten by a parent to the point of a mark being left on their body; and one in three couples engages in physical violence. A quarter of us grew up with alcoholic relatives, and one out of eight witnessed their mother being beaten or hit."[3]

With the pain, abuse, and neglect in our society, many faith skeptics ask the question: *"If God is perfect, why is there so much suffering in the world?"* I know this is a question many of you have in the back of your mind as well, so before we move on, may I have the privilege to address it?

We were created to live in a garden where sin and evil have no rule. In Genesis chapters 1 and 2, God lovingly created the world, the environment, and His children as He desired. He created a perfect garden where His beloved, made in His image, could live without shame and guilt (naked and pure).

He supplied more than enough provision to meet all their needs. God, the Father, would walk with Adam and Eve in the "cool of the day," where a relationship with God was nurtured, and identity and purpose were affirmed. Everything that Adam and Eve wanted and needed was overflowing in abundance. There were no voids.

There was just one thing that God asked. He placed one boundary. Adam and Eve could partake of anything in the garden except the "tree of the knowledge of good and evil" as mentioned in Genesis 2:17.

Why would God place one boundary, one tree, and one restriction? God gave Adam and Eve the gift of choice. True love is not truly love without a choice. God did not force Adam and Eve to love and choose Him. He gave them the choice. Their choice brought the consequences of sin and evil into our world today.

We have a choice as well. We can choose to yield to God, His boundaries, and reject sin, or we can choose to believe the lie that God is withholding something, and there is a better way. Our choices for sin, along with other people's choices to sin against us, bring pain and wounding into our lives. God has always desired only good things for us. Sin got in the way and still gets in the way. God hates sin, and yet still gives us the choice to choose our way or His way.

Satan, the enemy, came to Adam and Eve in the form of a serpent and whispered a lie. He accused God of withholding good things from His created children. God gave them all their hearts needed and desired, but the accusation was that God was not enough.

This was the same lie the Israelites believed when wandering in the desert. (Exodus 16:8) It was also the same untruth presented to Jesus Himself when he was tempted in the wilderness by Satan. (Luke 4:1-13) The same tactic was used when Jesus shares the Parable of the Talents, where the wicked servant buried his talent because - "he thought the Master to be a harsh ruler." (Matthew 25:24) This is the same lie presented to us when we think God's ways are antiquated, and He is trying to hold us back from something better.

So, let me be clear: God does not bring harm into our lives. Sin and the enemy bring pain and trauma into our lives. The enemy's goal is to inflict trauma through any open door in early childhood to stifle and stunt a person's *FLOW* of health and wholeness. The earlier in life this happens, the more destructive the damage because the child does not have the understanding, skills, or maturity to process it properly. Let me again clarify God does not cause these horrific things to happen to you. He hates them! This sinful, fallen world and sinful choices people make are to blame. Sin opens the door to the enemy to steal, kill, and destroy.

Let's not switch the cards, but remember the enemy is the deceiver. If you want to get angry at someone, you can get angry at the one who whispers the lies: the devil. You can use your anger to reclaim what the enemy stole from you.

Because of Jesus' death and resurrection on the cross, we have the keys of victory and authority over the devil. Let's assert our authority and push the enemy out. Remember, we have a choice. We have the authority to silence those whispering lies when they come to stop the sin cycle and choose life.

Now that it is clear God is not the source of trauma, I want to take the rest of this chapter to continue discussing the effects of trauma.

Although I have personally experienced trauma, once again, I am not an expert on the topic. I will share my experiences and quote the research of other experts who have spent a lifetime researching the topic, such as Bessel Van Der Kolk. Trauma is layered, and the impacts can be imprinted on every cell of the body. Van Der Kolk says, "Research has revealed that trauma produces actual physiological changes, including recalibration of the brain's alarm system, an increase in stress hormone activity, and alterations in the system that filters relevant information from irrelevant information."[4] It's no wonder that people who have experienced trauma have a more difficult time *FLOW*ing with a healthy heart.

For example, when we have experienced trauma, a normal event can be misinterpreted and trigger the body's alarm system to signal at the highest level. This alarming causes the executive function in our brain to disengage. The pituitary gland is signaled and communicates the need for defense and protection to our entire body. Our body is triggered and alarmed. The traumatized brain takes over; it partially shuts down the higher brain, leading to an irrational response to a normal situation. Have you ever seen someone completely overreact in a grocery store, at school, or public place? Who knows what traumatic event in their life triggered a reaction which shut down executive function and caused them to self-protect?

To neglect discussing the effects of trauma while talking about living a life of internal health and *FLOW* would be be irresponsible. Many times, it is the triggered trauma that alarms our brains to respond and lead us into unhealthy patterns. Acknowledging where there has been trauma is the first step to our healing.

I have experienced multiple traumatic events myself. My counselor once called it emotional polytrauma. These multiple traumatic events have given me a sensitive nervous system. Please don't jump out and scare me...ever! I will jump five feet off the ground, punch you in your face, and scream so loud the neighbors will call 911. My nervous system requires gentle care as a result of trauma.

I am being healed more and more every day. I am stronger and more resilient than ever, but I respect my limits and needs. What one person may be fine with, I may not be. I have learned to be content knowing that my weakness makes me further lean into Christ's strength. The apostle Paul said, *"But my grace is sufficient for you, for my power is made perfect in weakness."* (2 Corinthians 12:9, NIV) Paul was saying when we experience areas where we are fragile and vulnerable, Christ's power will give us the grace to carry on and move forward.

In my twenties, I desired to give my whole life to God in ministry. I did not "just date" anyone. I wanted to be with someone who had the same desires to love God and serve Him. At the age of 24, I married a newly-saved young man who was passionate about Jesus, but was not healed emotionally or discipled by other godly men.

Three months into the marriage, I realized I was being severely emotionally abused. Divorce was never an option in my mind. I am an extremely loyal person. More than that, I love and fear the Lord and His Ways. I would rather fail in any other area in life than the area God deems a holy reflection of who He is. Marriage is holy. The sanctity of marriage should be held in the highest honor and considered holy, according to the Bible. I understood this sanctity, and fought for my marriage with every fiber of my being.

The abuse was so severe that I lost 25 pounds from my already slim frame. I looked like walking skin and bones. Daily, I woke up in pain and went to bed in pain. The rejection was beyond anything I could bear. It was demonic. I had to make some difficult decisions. I knew God didn't condone divorce. I also knew God didn't create people to endlessly endure severe abuse. As I mentioned earlier, another person's sin brought trauma into my life. (I am not talking about getting your feelings hurt from inconsideration. I am talking about severe abuse.)

I was divorced after just a couple of years of marriage. It felt like the biggest failure of my life, and it was a failure I didn't choose. The record of being divorced still follows me on legal documents to this day, although my former husband is now deceased.

I am so grateful for forgiveness, healing from trauma, and God's grace and goodness. After several years, the Lord's love brought significant healing to my heart and my husband, Jon. I courageously moved forward in our marriage, although I was afraid.

The combination of the triggered trauma in me and Jon's experiences in relationships gave more opportunity for pain. I would wake up in the middle of the night with dreams that Jon was breaking up with me a decade after being married, all due to trauma. When I awoke, I panicked because it felt so real. These tormenting dreams would happen many times per week.

The lack of understanding about trauma, mixed with the whispering lies of the enemy, hindered my healing. Cycles of trauma continued until a project required Jon to study trauma. God is good and faithful! Sigh of relief here. Through his study, he was able to understand what I had been through, then bring validation of my experience and become an agent of healing instead of being a hindrance. He learned that one of the most important things you can do for a person who has experienced trauma is to validate their experience, even if you disagree with the reaction to it or don't understand it.

After Jon and I were married six months, I became pregnant with our first son, Joseph. When Joseph was six months old, I became pregnant with our second son, Josiah. We decided I would stay home with our two strong-willed boys immediately after marriage since they were so close together.

I am a people-person, goal-oriented, and an Enneagram three, the Achiever. But I felt like I was not able to achieve anything. I worked all day to see only little results by evening. (Mom life!) I was going in circles all day, achieving seemingly nothing. (I know it was not true, but it was how I felt day-after-day.) This was difficult for me because of the dissonance between how I was designed by God coupled with the insecure feelings while I was at home all day. I could navigate one or the other, but the two meshed together with long, exhausting days home alone with strong-willed children made it extreme. The combination of both of these factors for extended years was traumatic for me.

I was so grateful I was at home with our boys because more trauma invaded my life when our oldest son, Joseph, developed brain cancer at four years old. Our lives stopped. We fought for Joseph's life with everything in us, then he passed away from this earth just five months later.

I am now grateful I was with him in those long days even though they were hard. I have no regrets. We spent hours at the park, running errands, and singing songs in the car together. I soaked up every second of his life and I am thankful for those hard days now. I can now look back and see the grace of staying home with my boys because God knew the number of Joseph's days.

Just imagine the survival mode I was in. I was healing from the abuse from the first marriage, coping with a lack of understanding of my emotions in my second marriage, not using my gifts in a way I was designed, while simultaneously fighting for my son's life and grieving his death. Well, that was a lot of trauma to put into one sentence!

You have seen how trauma can keep us running in circles and repeating cycles. So what do we do to heal from our trauma? To heal from trauma is a long process, and there may be repetitive triggers to navigate. I want to assure you there is hope and healing from trauma.

Trauma does not have to end in tragedy!

Healing from the imprints of trauma

Professionals of study in this area reveal to heal from trauma, a person practically needs the following:

43

1. To learn what to do when triggered.

2. To learn how to become self-aware. (Honoring the truth of your emotions. Noticing annoyance, anxiety, and nervousness immediately helps to shift the automatic reaction by renewing the mind and responding to it instead of reacting to it.)

3. To have a supportive network of relationships. Research proves over and over again this is the single most powerful protection against becoming traumatized and for healing of trauma. Traumatized human beings recover in the context of safe relationships.

4. Movement. (Dance, stretching, walking, biking, exercise)

5. Physical touch. (Massage, hugs, hands on shoulder from safe people)

6. Reframe the traumatic event. (Instead of thinking of yourself as a victim, process the event by acknowledging you were victimized, but you are not a victim in every area of life. It was not your fault. (EMDR therapy, Restoring the Foundations Ministry, trauma counseling, etc.)

I want to add the spiritual component as well. People who have experienced trauma need:

1. To receive God's love daily. God's love heals. Remember, God is not the author of trauma.

2. To renew their mind in the Word of God daily. Find a simple Bible reading plan and read it daily.

3. To receive deliverance from demonic oppression that resulted from the trauma.

4. To declare and decree the truth out loud regularly. "*You will also declare a thing, and it will be established for you.*" Job 22:28 (NKJV) Write out Scriptures and truths of who you are in Christ.

Van Der Kolk says, "More than anything else, being able to be safe with other people defines mental health; safe connections are fundamental to meaningful and satisfying lives."[5] There is no simple formula for healing when polytrauma has occurred in a person's life. Intentional attention is needed, and patience is required.

The process I share to *FLOW* again in this book is a beginning step for those who have experienced deep trauma. Because Scripture backs this process, I firmly believe it is a step in the right direction to unlock the *FLOW* in any person's heart.

Let's take some time now to identify possible traumatic events that may have occurred in your life. This is a time to not overlook anything, but to honestly acknowledge harmful events that have shaped you, even if it seems not as monumental as others. Events earlier in our lives have a tremendous effect on us, so pay close attention to occurrences in your childhood. Ask the Holy Spirit to help you identify any part of your life you need to acknowledge.

Identify any painful or traumatic experience that happened in each season of your life next.

Before you were born (A parent's or grandparent's trauma which may have affected you.):

_____

_____

_____

_____

Birth to five years:

_____

_____

_____

_____

Six to twelve years:

_____

_____

_____

_____

Thirteen to eighteen years:

_____

_____

_____

_____

Nineteen to twenty-five years:

_____

_____

_____

_____

Twenty-five to forty years old:

_____

_____

_____

_____

Forty years and older:

_____

_____

_____

_____

Awareness and processing of early trauma are imperative to living with a healthy heart. I am praying the Holy Spirit reveals areas that need attention now. I will see you in chapter 4 to explain the *FLOW* process from Psalm 139 to unlock the hindrances that can keep you stifled.

Chapter 4

Getting Unstuck: Cultivating Your FLOW

"O Lord, you have examined my heart and know everything about me."

Psalm 139:1 (NLT)

Life's hurts and traumas can cause intense heart pain, making us resistant to trust others, and sometimes even God. As a result, our hearts become kinked, cutting off the *FLOW* and even the voice of the Holy Spirit, which is trying to guide our lives.

In this chapter of the book, we will learn how to restore that heart *FLOW* so we can commune with God again as He intended.

The pathway is simple. It literally can be broken down into a four-step process using the acronym F.L.O.W. from Psalm 139:1-24.

- **F** - Filter Your Thoughts and Emotions

- **L** - Let God Love You

- **O** - Order Your Thoughts

- **W** - Willingly Repent

I want to walk you through what it means to *FLOW* and how God teaches us about this process in the Bible when King David was struggling to heal his own heart pains in Psalm 139:11-12. The Bible refers to King David as "a man after God's own heart." (1 Sam. 13:14) That's high praise! Yet, if you read about David's life in 2 Samuel 12, he was by no means perfect.

He experienced profound heart pain throughout his life. He grew up in a highly dysfunctional family in which his own father didn't even consider him to be shown to the prophet Samuel as a candidate for king. David made many mistakes himself, such as sending a loyal soldier to his death so that David could cover the sin of infidelity with that man's wife.

However, one thing that David provided a good example of was quickly confessing his sins to the Lord and asking for forgiveness. Instead of defending his choices in pride, David was a professional repenter. David was a man after God's own heart not because of his stellar self-discipline and righteousness, but because of his humility.

In James 4:6b, the Bible tells us *"God opposes the proud but gives grace to the humble."* We see that played out in how God answered David's prayers in the psalms. As a result, we see God show up time and time again when David experienced deep pain in his life and, in Psalm 139, David outlines the four-step *FLOW* process to help us continue to heal the pains of the heart today. I will break down each part of the acronym as well.

As I have processed the pains in my life, it has always been intuitive for me to hash out my feelings with God. I would journal, and sometimes I would even end up yelling out to Him in frustration, trying to get to the root of how I felt. In those moments of unbearable pain, God's love would soothe me and His love would remind me of who I was. I would then naturally turn to the Scriptures to align my thoughts and feelings to God's ways.

As I have studied psychology, I have learned that processing our thoughts and feelings are part of healing. Instead of rehearsing the wrongs done over and over again, we choose to acknowledge it, then give it to God and break agreement with the lie associated with it. I observed where psychology confirmed Scripture and Scripture confirmed psychology.

I found the *FLOW* pattern in Psalm 139, and the lightbulb suddenly went off in my head. It confirmed my personal experiences and God was downloading a guide on how to tend my heart when life had been painful. I want to teach you to go through each step of this process so you can restore your heart's *FLOW*.

F - Filter Your Thoughts and Emotions

"O Lord, you have searched me and known me! You know when I sit down and when I rise up; you discern my thoughts from afar. You search out my path and my lying down and are acquainted with all my ways.

Even before a word is on my tounge, behold, O Lord, you know it altogether." Psalm 139:1-4

The first part to restoring *FLOW* in your life is to *filter your thoughts and emotions.* Life can move so swiftly that we rarely stop to acknowledge what we are feeling, much less believing. We are used to shoving our thoughts and emotions down without acknowledging them, sorting through them, asking if they are true, or if they are lies being whispered to us in the dark. Jeremiah 17:9 tells us, *"The heart is deceitful above all things, and desperately sick; who can understand it?"* Just because we think certain thoughts or feel certain emotions does not mean we join in agreement with them. It takes self-examination to know what is from God, what is from our enemy, what we need to change in the channel of our thoughts, and what we need to bring to the light to be healed.

Think about when you brew your coffee. You don't want the grounds going into your cup. You have to filter those out before you can enjoy that first sip. Similarly, if you like to organize like I do, sometimes we must sort through the clutter that accumulates and decide what must go and what can stay. Likewise, we must filter out the old, unwanted, or even harmful thoughts and emotions just like we filter unwelcome toxins and clutter from our bodies or homes.

However, it takes time to do this. You must honestly assess your feelings and your beliefs and take them captive like the Bible instructs in 2 Corinthians 10:4-5: *"For the weapons of our warfare are not of the flesh but have divine power to destroy strongholds. We destroy arguments and every lofty opinion raised against the knowledge of God, and take every thought captive to obey Christ."*

However, where I have found that sometimes Christians have problems with restoring *FLOW* is that we try to jump straight to faith and positive thinking without allowing ourselves to acknowledge valid pains and disappointments.

It is healthy to acknowledge how you feel. It is not healthy to ignore heart pains and stuff them down where they can fester and surface later on as bitterness, resentment, and mistrust. If you fail to address your true feelings, it can lead to being internally stuck and spiritually kinked, closing off your heart to the voice of God. Let's take a closer look at Psalm 139:1-4.

> *"O LORD, you have searched me and known me! You know when I sit down and when I rise up; you discern my thoughts from afar. You search out my path and my lying down and are acquainted with all my ways. Even before a word is on my tongue, behold, O LORD, you know it altogether."*

In this passage, not only is David setting up to unload his heart pains to God, but he understands and acknowledges that God already knows all the gunk in his heart. We forget that God knows our thoughts and emotions better than we do. Sometimes we are blind to our own thoughts and emotions. We don't see what is buried under the surface until we allow time for God to illuminate the truth to us. At other times, we can be afraid of acknowledging our true feelings for fear of disappointing God and forget He is not only well aware of them, but welcomes our honesty. He is waiting for us to come to Him and confess the hurts we have been tightly grasping so He can remove the weight of them. We were never intended to shoulder the pains of life alone by shoving down our emotions.

After Jon and I lost our son, Joseph, to cancer, we were faced with many well-meaning Christians who unknowingly invalidated our grieving with Scriptures. I know most of them were well-intentioned and trying to spare us pain by focusing our eyes on the truth we already knew, that our son was in heaven. But unless you have lost a child, you cannot begin to understand the overwhelming heart pain we were experiencing. Even with the solid faith and foundation we both had in Jesus, there was no Scripture to help us magically skip over the pain of that loss. It had to be processed.

Eventually, we had to stop running from it and face it head on. We had to embrace the pain and go through the season of mourning. There were times when it was really ugly and difficult. I chose to acknowledge the vulnerability of the loss and pain I was feeling, as well as my desire to put up walls of self-protection. Then I began sorting through my honest thoughts. I had to present the thoughts and emotions that would bubble up to God. As they did, I began to train my brain to filter them according to God's Word so I could move into step two of the *FLOW* process and learn to receive His love again.

L - Let God Love You

"You hem me in, behind and before, and lay your hand upon me. Such knowledge is too wonderful for me; it is high; I cannot attain it. Where shall I go from your Spirit? Or where shall I flee from your presence? If I ascend to heaven, you are there! If I make my bed in Sheol, you are there! If I take the wings of the morning and dwell in the uttermost parts of the sea, even there your hand shall lead me, and your right hand shall hold me. If I say, 'Surely the darkness shall cover me, and the light about me be night,' even the darkness

Flow: Keeping Your Heart Alive When Life Hurts

is not dark to you; the night is bright as the day, for darkness isas light with you. For you formed my inward parts; you knitted me together in my mother's womb. I praise you, for I am fearfully and wonderfully made. Wonderful are your works; my soul knows it very well. My frame was not hidden from you, when I was being made in secret, intricately woven in the depths of the earth. Your eyes saw my unformed substance; in your book were written, every one of them, the days that were formed for me, when as yet there was none of them. How precious to me are your thoughts, O God! How vast is the sum of them! If I would count them, they are more than the sand. I awake, and I am still with you." Psalm 139:5-18

When you are hurting, it can be easy to wall yourself off from others so that they cannot hurt you anymore. However, when you do this, you forget that those walls are not only keeping out pain, but they are keeping out love as well.

After I began to filter my thoughts and emotions, I realized that even though I was crying out to God to help me heal from the pain of losing Joseph, I was not letting God's love in. When God showed me this, it struck a chord because, as a parent, one of the things I love most is when my children let me hold them and love on them. How much more so does God, as the perfect parent, want to love on us?

If you have children, you know how frustrating it can be when your child doesn't want to sit still and let you hold them, especially when they're hurting. Yet, that is what I was doing to God. I was so consumed by the pain of my heart that I had walled myself off to receiving the healing love of my Heavenly Father.

55

In Psalm 139:7-12, David reminds us that, even in his pain, God was always there. He is omnipresent, present *every-where*, even in our pain. We have to come to the place where we let the light of that healing presence back into our closed off hearts:

> "*Where shall I go from your Spirit? Or where shall I flee from your presence? If I ascend to heaven, you are there! If I make my bed in Sheol, you are there! If I take the wings of the morning and dwell in the uttermost parts of the sea, even there your hand shall lead me, and your right hand shall hold me. If I say, 'Surely the darkness shall cover me, and the light about me be night,' even the darkness is not dark to you; the night is bright as the day, for darkness is as light with you.*" Psalm 139:7-12

When you allow God to show you who you are in Him and you let Him love you, nothing can stop you. It doesn't matter what people say or think about you because your identity in Christ is immovable. God's love is able to bring peace to your heart and soothe your mind, as it settles deep within you. God's peace is right there waiting for us to receive it. It does not move. It chases us no matter how far we try to run or how much we close our hearts due to the traumas and pains of life. Why then, is it sometimes so difficult for us to receive that perfect, healing love?

As Jon and I began to really study trauma therapy and dig into the Bible together to discover where Scripture and psychology overlapped, one theory I observed had to do with developmental attachment and how we experience love from a very young age. Even children who are raised by loving parents in healthy families struggle with receiving love because we are imperfect humans. Only God is capable of perfect love. He designed us to need His love.

That kind of sounds like an oxymoron, right? How can you learn to receive love from God if you've maybe never properly attached to humans in a healthy way? I consider myself to have come from a loving family. It wasn't perfect, but my mother was a nurturer. She was always there. My father was a hard worker who didn't really know how to process emotions, but he was always there. I was raised to love God from an early age, but it wasn't until I *experienced* God's love that it became real to me.

When I was six years old, I had a very real encounter with God. I was going to sleep and, as I was saying my nightly prayers, I laid my hand out and said, "God, if you're really real, I'm going to put my hand right here and I want you to lift it up. I'm not going to do anything." It sounds kind of silly, right? Yet, all of a sudden, I felt this tingling sensation in my hand, like there was oil dripping down it, and my hand lifted up not of my own accord but because I felt the hand of God wrap around mine. Whether or not you believe my account, it was such a powerful, supernatural sensation in my young life that I *knew* God was real. I quite literally felt His love. That sensation stays with me to this day.

When I went through my abusive first marriage where my ex-husband tried to use the Bible to shame me by comparing me to Leah, the unwanted wife of Jacob in the Bible, it was hard to remember that feeling and continue to receive God's love. My ex-husband would constantly remind me I was not enough. Even though I had won several beauty pageants and I had been raised in a loving home with a godly foundation, I began to believe the lies I was being told. I began to believe I was unlovable, ugly, and unwanted not just by my ex-husband, but by others too. It cut off my heart's *FLOW*.

Add to that the shame of going through a divorce knowing what the Bible says about divorce, I felt like I was irreparably damaged goods. I began to question the call to ministry that I felt God had given me when I was a teenager. I can remember getting into my car one day shortly after my divorce and yelling at God at the top of my lungs.

I was angry very much like David was when he cried out to God in Psalm 139:19-24:

> *"Oh that you would slay the wicked, O God! O men of blood, depart from me! They speak against you with malicious intent; your enemies take your name in vain. Do I not hate those who hate you, O LORD? And do I not loathe those who rise up against you? I hate them with complete hatred;I count them my enemies. Search me, O God, and know my heart! Try me and know my thoughts! And see if there be any grievous way in me, and lead me in the way everlasting!"*

Just as David unleashed his completely uncensored feelings to God in this passage, I followed his example that day in my car. Just as God drew David back with love, God drew me back, and He can draw you back too. In that moment after I had cried myself out, I felt God say, "*Joy, I see that you're hurting, and I see that you're in pain. This is wrong. It is unjust. It is not what I created you for, to be treated like this, but I am your safe place."* I had a choice to make: would I hold on to the heart hurt or would I learn how to let God love me again even though my identity and self-image had been shattered.

Friend, if you are in a place where you are wondering if you can ever learn to receive God's love based on the heart hurts, betrayals, and traumas you've endured in your life, I would encourage you to be honest with yourself and with God just like David did, just like I did. God would rather you yell at Him honestly about your inability to trust Him and receive His love.

He already knows what's in your heart and is bigger than your doubt. If you keep those lines of communication open and ask Him to help you learn to receive His love, I guarantee that He will meet you and teach you. He *is* love. If you ask Him, He will teach you how to let Him love you.

O - Order Your Thoughts

"Oh that you would slay the wicked, O God! O men of blood, depart from me! They speak against you with malicious intent; your enemies take your name in vain. Do I not hate those who hate you, O Lord? And do I not loathe those who rise up against you? I hate them with complete hatred; I count them my enemies." Psalm 139:19-22

When we filter our thoughts, we are identifying what is coming in and ruminating in our minds so we can begin to open our hearts to receiving God's love again. When we order our thoughts, we are letting God redirect our minds to replace the lies and hurts we were holding onto so tightly with His truth and healing. When we order our thoughts, we are doing what the Bible encourages us to do in Colossians 3:2, *"Set your minds on things that are above, not on things that are on earth."*

It can be difficult to surrender that control to God and let Him order your thoughts. It takes humility and being willing to get the old, negative thoughts up and out. We must be willing to tell God, *"not my will, but Yours be done."* (Luke 22:42) We acknowledge our thoughts and desires, then exchange them for His.

When you're hurting, it feels counterintuitive and vulnerable to trust someone else with that pain. But when you release that pain and give it to God, He offers a divine exchange of pain for peace.

You may be thinking, "Joy, how do you order your thoughts to get that divine exchange and restore *FLOW*?" It takes practice. It takes exercising those mental muscles. You have to make the decision to replace old thoughts with new ones and build an arsenal of healthy declarations upon which you speak out loud.

I have found memorization to be one of the best ways to do this. When I taught classical education, one of the core teachings is repetition and recitation to deeply ingrain what is being taught. Once it is ingrained, it can be recalled without effort. I don't have to even think about what the eight parts of speech are. They just come up because I have recited, chanted, and sung them countless times. I will never forget them. Just ask my students!

How much more so should we replace the old thought patterns with the Word of God? One of the best ways to do this and order your thoughts is to memorize Scripture. When the old thought patterns assault you and try to remind you of past trauma, you can combat them with the truth of God's Word. We can fight with the sword of the spirit in Eph. 6:17 on the battlefield that is constantly waging in our minds.

The Bible also says in Hebrews 4:12: "*The word of God is living and active, sharper than any two-edged sword, piercing to the division of soul and of spirit, of joints and of marrow, and discerning the thoughts and intentions of the heart.*" It is a tool that the devil doesn't want us to learn to use because he knows how powerful it is.

The more you read God's Word and align your thoughts to what the Bible says, it becomes embedded in your mind and ready to help you fight when you need it. It will bring your thoughts up higher and remodel how you walk, talk, think, and act. Again, none of these steps are easy at first. Traumas can create serious strongholds in your mind and your heart that take time and immense focus to break down. It takes consistent effort, but it is so worth it.

As I've said before, we do not always get to choose what happens to us in life, but we *can* choose how we respond to it. We can choose if we will let it defeat us and keep us stuck or if we will allow God to restore the *FLOW* of our hearts. The more proficient you are at taking your thoughts captive to the truth of God, then speaking out loud those truths, the more freedom and *FLOW* will be manifested in your heart and life.

David did this in Psalm 119:11 NLT where he writes, "*I have hidden your word in my heart, that I might not sin against you.*" David knew that his strength to fight against the negative thoughts and the hurts of life could be found in the Word of God. He knew that he had to memorize and use Scripture to order his thoughts and align them in ways that would keep his heart flowing and pure.

The more you align your thoughts with God's Word, the more you will see God without the cloudiness of sin that can blur your view and keep you stuck. When you live with purity of heart, you can recognize the truth of God's Word about yourself and your situation easier. It is in your rote memory and has carved new pathways in your brain because you have trained your brain to think differently.

You may be wondering why I keep dwelling on sin here. After all, we have been talking about how to restore your heart *FLOW* because you have been the victim of pain. I want you to take a deep breath and stay with me because we are about to dive into perhaps the most important part of the *FLOW* process, but also the most difficult.

We have learned how to filter our negative thoughts and emotions, let God's love in, and order our thoughts to come in agreement with God's truth. Now we have to also recognize the part we have played and willingly repent.

W - Willingly Repent

"Search me, O God, and know my heart! Try me and know my thoughts! And see if there be any grievous way in me, and lead me in the way everlasting!" Psalm 139:23-24

I want to pause right here because I know the initial visceral reaction women usually give me when they see the phrase *willingly repent*. "Joy! I'm the victim here! My heart has been put through the blender. *I've* been betrayed. People have hurt *me*. Why on earth do *I* have to repent?" Friend, I am so glad you asked. It is different from what you expect, and it goes against everything inside of you.

But if you don't face the part you played in harboring resentment, unforgiveness, bitterness, and even victimization, God cannot free you. You have to release those negative feelings keeping you bound before God can flood your soul with freedom. When you willingly repent, you are telling God, "*I am at the end of myself. I no longer want to play judge. Your will be done. I trust You.*" Those are the hardest but most freeing words you can pray.

The willing repentance step in this process did not feel natural. It did not feel normal to willingly repent for my offenses. If I forgave and released that person or situation, it seemed like I was excusing what happened. What I learned was I did not need to excuse the situation, I needed to hand it over to the real judge of the situation. That is God's job, if we let Him do it. The last step in the *FLOW* process is what bursts open the freedom. Once I took this step of faith, the stifled places inside unleashed.

I didn't realize when I married Jon how I had carried so much of the pain, mistrust, trauma triggers, and general lies of the enemy endured from my first marriage into my new relationship. It was probably ten years into my marriage to Jon before I realized and acknowledged I was holding on to toxic thought patterns that were harming our relationship.

I had not yet gone on this *FLOW* journey.

It's funny because even looking back at the night he proposed to me, I was trying to trauma bomb him and talk him out of wanting to marry me! As we were sitting at dinner together, all of my insecurities of having been told I was a Leah, not a Rachel, and that I wasn't enough, came flooding back to the forefront of my mind. I was scared to death. I thank God that Jon and I were both seeking the Holy Spirit that night because later we discovered that we were both asking the Holy Spirit the same questions: *"What do I do? Do I move forward? Do I pull back?"* We both felt the Holy Spirit leading us to move forward, but I was panicking because I was extra sensitive due to my trauma. I had not yet learned how to let my heart be healed.

It took therapy, prayer, rebuking the lies of the enemy, journaling, memorizing, and declaring Scripture to move forward. I had to take every thought captive and let both God and Jon love me. Then there ultimately came that moment where I had to willingly come to the end of trying to protect myself. I chose to surrender and willingly repent of my role of having accepted the lies I had been told. I had to order my thoughts in a new way and affirm a new identity that I was not rejected but beautiful in God's eyes. I had to receive forgiveness from God for my unhealthy thought patterns I had allowed to take root for so long.

There is a massive degree of humility required to come to this place. David, the professional repenter, said, *"Search me, O God, and know my heart; test me and know my anxious thoughts. Point out anything in me that offends you, and lead me along the path of everlasting life"* (Psalm 139:23-24 NLT).

Humility is a secret superpower that allows God to point out anything in us that is not of Him so He can heal it. But it is not easy to self-examine and bring those hidden heart pains and personal shortcomings up to the light where we have to look closely at them. At this place of healing, professional counseling can be helpful to get us out of our own heads and help us see things about ourselves from new angles so that we can finally heal.

No one likes to expose their weaknesses or have their faults pointed out, but that is the only way God can wash us clean of them. Humility is what compelled David to repent quickly every time he was confronted with sin because he didn't want this sin to keep him kinked and separated from God. Humility says, "*Not my way, but your way, God.*"

When we can honestly say, "*Search me, God,*" we invite God to heal us like David did in Psalm 51:10: "*Create in me a pure heart, O God, and renew a steadfast spirit within me.*" When you willingly repent like David did, it breaks open the dam that has been keeping your heart kinked so that the healing waters can burst forth and restore your heart's *FLOW*.

Willingly repenting is the most powerful step in the entire *FLOW* process. You cannot restore *FLOW* without it! Filtering your thoughts and emotions, letting God love you, and ordering your steps are all part of the process and good in so many ways, but unless you repent of trying to wrestle control away from God, you will not be free.

Repentance is the key to freedom!

You must reach that point of surrender, but you must also do it willingly. God is not going to force you. He is patient and he is ready for you when you decide to take this massive step of faith and trust. But it has to come from a place of willingness, and seeing there are no other options. You are not powerful enough to do it in your own strength. Nor were you designed to do so.

It doesn't mean that the situation or the pain will resolve itself. It does mean you are allowing God to come in where the enemy has walled off your heart so He can make it soft and whole again.

In the coming chapters, we will look at how to topically apply this *FLOW* process to some of life's most common heart pains so that you can get free of whatever is keeping your heart kinked. Whether it's disappointment and unmet expectations, resentment or bitterness, feelings of rejection, betrayals by people you trusted, anger at the injustices of the world, or loss and grief of a loved one, this *FLOW* process can be applied to free you and let God heal your heart.

It doesn't mean the situation or pain will resolve itself. I can't promise it will be easy. I can pretty much guarantee you will encounter some of those traumas head-on, but friend, I have been where you are. I have faced all of these issues and I would not be writing this book if I did not know without a shadow of a doubt that God can heal you and restore your *FLOW*. We are in this together. Let's break down those barriers. Here are some questions to ask yourself as you allow God to begin restoring your heart *FLOW*. We will use this process in the coming chapters for the various types of heart pains you may be facing.

1. **Filter Your Thoughts and Emotions.** Take inventory of what you are thinking and feeling at this moment. Be honest with yourself. What thoughts are revolving in your heart and mind?

2. **Let God Love You.** What are you believing about yourself? What does God say about you as His child whom He loves dearly?

3. **Order Your Thoughts.** How can you take the harmful and negative thoughts coming from yourself, your circumstances, other people, the enemy, or even God and align them with God's Word?

4. **Willingly Repent.** Take a moment to repent and ask God to cleanse you of allowing those heart kinks to stop the *FLOW* of His Holy Spirit. Ask God to restore His *FLOW* so you can freely hear His voice and accept His love, allowing your heart to heal.

Declaration

Let's boldly declare this paraphrased portion of Psalm 139 to re-affirm our identity as a beloved child of God.

God, I can never escape your presence and your perfect love. If I go to high places or low places, you promise your love follows me. You will be behind me and guiding me back toward the light of your loving presence. You formed the uniqueness of my personality, mind, and body. You created me wonderfully. Nothing about me is a mistake. I am wonderfully complex just as you intended. Thank you for weaving me together perfectly in your image. Help me to learn to love who you created me to be and accept who I am completely in you. Your thoughts toward me are precious and too many to count. Every morning, when I wake up, help me to recognize that you are there no matter how I feel in the moment. Help me to remind myself that you look at me and are proud of who I am. I am loved today and every day by you.

Chapter 5

Rejecting Rejection

"No person's rejection can ever exempt me from God's love for me. Period."[6]

Lysa Terkeurst

Rejection tried to label me from inside the womb. Generational rejection passed down to me was in my DNA. As a child I was a little unsure of myself. Although I was well-liked by my peers, I had this gnawing sense that something was wrong with me. I felt that if people could see me up close, they would know and run away. Rejection demanded that I kept the shining smile and good performance, but kept real vulnerability and intimacy with others out. As long as I looked good and was fed praises from others, I accepted myself. But as soon as I underperformed and someone saw my faults, I would fall to pieces. I did not believe I was unconditionally loved when I messed up. It's easy to hide rejection when you can outperform everyone else, but it is easily exposed when you can't.

I remember playing in a high school basketball game during a poor performance streak. I made one last bad pass when I ran off the court crying like a toddler to the locker room in the middle of a game. My identity was attached to my performance, looks, grades, and accomplishments. I lived under the spell of rejection for most of my life until I broke this entrapment of a stronghold.

This childhood rejection made me vulnerable to an abusive marriage and abusive people and systems. The rejection in my soul and the generational tendencies passed to me were a magnet for abusive treatment. When I truly believed that my lovable identity as a daughter of God is confirmed and not determined by my performance, weight, smooth skin, or letters behind my name, I could relax and breathe.

I finally accepted myself for who I truly was. As a child of God, I have everything I need and no one else can define who I am. My identity in Christ shapes everything about me and my uniqueness makes me set apart for God's glory. You, my friend, are one-of-a-kind too! You can accept and love yourself as perfectly designed - a masterpiece.

Rejection and trauma tried to take out my friend, Kelli. The abrupt isolation during COVID-19 left Kelli feeling lonely and triggered. During this challenging time, pain erupted like a volcano from her heart. All of the years of shoving her emotions down could no longer be restrained during the isolation. Her heart unraveled. The confinement of COVID-19 brought

Kelli back to her first memory as a child when she was home alone watching headlights drive up to her house. She feared Child Protective Services was coming to take her away. Being alone always scared Kelli.

Kelli's mother battled severe mental illness. Her father was distant. Her household was brimming with screaming, put-downs, blaming, and abandonment. Sometimes her mother would vanish for days. In her absence, echoes of stinging words like, "I should have had an abortion" left Kelli feeling rejected and afraid. The trauma of her mother being hospitalized nearly 50 times during her childhood was deeply embedded in Kelli's body, spirit, and soul. Abuse, abandonment, and absence were common in her early years. Still, Kelli found a way to suppress and survive.

As Kelli grew older, she met and fell in love with Jesus, making Him her Lord. Jesus was her everything. She found security in His love. Kelli even became a small group leader at church. She refused to live with a victim mindset any longer.

Then COVID-19 stormed the stage of her life. She realized during the COVID-19 lockdown that she had never acknowledged the hurt and rejection of her childhood. The excruciating void was still lurking in the crevices of her heart, waiting for the right trigger to bring it to center stage. The rejection from her past became all-consuming, affecting her daily life. A depression with just the right amount of relational voids led to a suicide attempt. This tragic experience forced Kelli to acknowledge her pain, seek proper help, and find healing.

Kelli is an overcomer. She did the work and faced the pain. She allowed God to love her and ordered her thoughts to the Word of God. Kelli forgave those who abused her. While not excusing what they did, she released them to the Father's justice. Kelli is victorious and continues to move forward with her life. She is now enrolled in college, facing her fears, and being honest with herself. She is pursuing God's love and freedom in her life.

As we read through the Bible, we see many other people who have faced rejection. Many biblical heroes of faith have faced rejection, such as Joseph, Hagar, and the prophet Jeremiah. Yet, in all Scripture, no one endured more than Jesus. The rejection Jesus faced was unfathomable. Jesus tasted deep rejection, not unlike what you or I have experienced.

Jesus faced rejection from His family, friends, followers, community, and briefly from the Father Himself as He hung on the cross. Through His rejection, Jesus paved the way for us to face our own. Jesus' own brothers did not believe in Him. (John 7:5) He was without honor in His hometown. He could not do mighty works in the town of His family because of their unbelief. (Matthew 15:57-58)

Jesus knows what it is like to be rejected by those closest to Him. Judas, one of the twelve disciples of Jesus, betrayed Him in the end. Rejection from those closest to us can be the worst kind of rejection. Jesus hung on the cross in His darkest moment. It was here He expressed the rejection He felt as He cried out, *"My God, my God, why have you forsaken me?"* (Matthew 27:46) Jesus was taking on the rejection of all the world - your rejection and mine.

It is easier to tolerate criticism and rejection from distant people. It is harder from those we love the most, like a spouse, parents, family, or close friend. Rejection from immediate family members can be painful. This is especially true when rejection affects a child like Kelli. She did not have the skills to process the rejection, so she believed she was defective and unwanted. She felt that her core identity had been damaged.

Kelli's parents criticized and rejected her. Parental rejection can occur when a parent is never in the picture, when a parent leaves the family, or when disinterest and dishonor define the home. Any child can be vulnerable to a spirit of rejection that whispers, "*You are unworthy. You are defective. You are not acceptable. You are unwanted.*" How can a child defend himself or herself from these pain-filled beliefs and feelings? As the child grows and matures, he or she can live a life operating from this spirit, or embrace a new identity in Christ. You can dismantle the spirit of rejection operating as a stronghold in your mind and heart like Kelli did.

We must understand the source of rejection. At the root of all rejection is the underworking force of our enemy, the devil. Remember Jesus' riveting words in John 10:10, "*The thief comes only to steal and kill and destroy. I came that they may have life and have it abundantly.*"

Rejection can come from childhood or teenage friends, school, and even well-meaning people. When we believe and agree with the voice of rejection, we experience defeat. We can choose not to agree with the voice of rejection and instead agree with the Spirit of God. In Christ, we are not rejected but chosen. We have an identity from Him as sons and daughters of a living God. What does He say about us? "*When my father and mother forsake me, then the Lord will take care of me.*" Psalm 27:10 (NKJV)

In Genesis 29, we meet Leah in the Bible who was completely rejected by her husband, Jacob. Let's pause and read Genesis 29 now for context.

Jacob did not even want to marry Leah. He wanted to marry her younger sister, Rachel, but their father switched the bride and tricked Jacob into marrying Leah because she was older. What was her father thinking? He was so desperate for Leah, the older sister, to get married he didn't realize how much pain this would cause in his family and to Leah personally. In those times having a husband was the only means of provision for women. I'm sure Leah's father thought he was helping her by manipulating a marriage for her.

What does Genesis 29:31 reveal about God's heart for those who have been rejected?

_____

_____

_____

Read Genesis 29:32-35. How many sons did Leah have by this time?

_____

_____

_____

Read Genesis 30:1-24. Who all experienced rejection in this chapter?

_____

_____

_____

_____

What did Rachel and Leah both do when they each felt rejection?

_____

_____

_____

_____

Where should we take our rejection?

_____

_____

_____

_____

Remember, I was literally referred to as Leah by my first husband. How awful is that? I know now that the enemy, Satan, was at the root of this, but at the time, I felt like I was defective, ugly, and unlovable. I went from beauty queen to "Leah" in a few years. Thank goodness I am not defined by circumstances or people, and neither are you. Thankfully, I was able to heal from the wounds of rejection in my life. I am loved today so extravagantly by my husband and my boys. I am the queen of my house and am told how beautiful I am every day. God knew having a household of all boys celebrating me and loving me would bring truth to exterminate the lie that Satan used to try to destroy me. I am not rejected or unlovable, but the opposite.

You are not rejected or unlovable either. What circumstances in your life have caused you to agree with the spirit and voice of rejection? What rejection is coming to your mind right now? Who has turned on you? What situations made you feel rejected? Maybe the rejection is subtle and not obvious to others. Maybe your family was great, but you have rejected yourself. Perhaps you put unrealistic expectations on yourself that were not meant for you to wear. Like Leah, maybe your spouse rejected you. Rejection is not your identity as a child of God.

I am praying for you now as you go through the *FLOW* process to unlock your heart. I am asking the Holy Spirit to guide you as you uncover obvious or hidden places of rejection in your heart.

Let's filter the rejection you have experienced now.

1. Filter your thoughts and emotions.

What rejection is the Holy Spirit bringing up right now? Write your first thought.

_____

_____

_____

What are some other areas and situations where you have encountered rejection?

_____

_____

_____

What thoughts about this rejection circulate in your mind and your emotions?

_____

_____

_____

_____

_____

What are you believing about yourself as a result of the rejection you have faced?

_____

_____

_____

_____

_____

How are you acting and behaving as a result of this rejection?

_____

_____

_____

_____

_____

2. Let God love you.

What does God think about you? (Read Psalm 139 again.)

_____

_____

_____

_____

Look up Psalm 34:18. Where is God with the rejection you are facing right now?

_____

_____

_____

_____

_____

Allow the Holy Spirit to speak truth to you personally now. Ask Him to tell you how much He loves you.

_____

_____

_____

_____

Now declare this paraphrase from Psalm 139 aloud.

I can never escape your presence and love! Whether I go to high places or low places, your love will pursue me. Even when I go to dark places, you will follow me and bring me to the light. You formed the uniqueness of my personality, mind, and body. I am wonderfully created just as you intended. Nothing about me is a mistake. Thank you for making me wonderfully complex! You wove me together perfectly how you liked. I like what you created and accept who I am completely. Your thoughts toward me are precious and too many to count. Every morning when I wake up you are there, no matter how I feel. You look at me and are proud of who I am. I am loved today and every day by You!

3. Order your thoughts.

"As a man thinks in his heart, so he is." Proverbs 23:7

Use the following Scriptures to write your own personal declaration to order your thoughts to the truth and resist a spirit of rejection.

"Be strong and courageous, Do not be afraid or terrified because of them, for the Lord goes with you; he will never leave you or forsake you." Deuteronomy 31:6

"I remain confident of this: I will see the goodness of the Lord in the land of the living." Psalm 27:13

"Though my father and mother forsake me, the Lord will hold me close." Psalm 27:10

"As you come to Him, the living Stone - rejected by humans but chosen by God and precious to Him." 1 Peter 2:4

"Can a mother forget the baby at her breast and have no compassion on the child she has born? Though she may forget, I will not forget you." Isaiah 49:15

"If the world hates you, keep in mind that it hated Me first." John 15:18

"For the Lord will not reject His people; He will never forsake His inheritance." Psalm 94:14

"Therefore, there is now no condemnation for those who are in Christ Jesus." Romans 8:1

"What, then, shall we say in response to these things? If God is for us, who can be against us." Romans 8:31

"'For I know the plans I have for you,' declares the Lord, 'plans to prosper you and not to harm you, plans to give you hope and a future.'" Jeremiah 29:11

"But He said to me, 'My grace is sufficient for you, for My power is made perfect in weakness.' Therefore I will boast all the more gladly about my weaknesses, so that Christ's power may rest on me." 2 Corinthians 12:9

"Truly my soul finds rest in God; my salvation comes from Him. Truly He is my rock and my salvation; He is my fortress, I will never be shaken." Psalm 62:1-2

"For you did not receive the spirit of bondage again to fear, but you received the Spirit of adoption by whom we cry out, 'Abba, Father.'"
Romans 8:15

Here is an example of a declaration:

I am a child of God. I am fearfully and wonderfully made. Although some humans have rejected me, God has not forsaken or rejected me. I am wonderfully made. Even if my mother or father fails me, God will not fail me. Even if a spouse, friend, or family member rejects me, I am accepted and dearly loved by God. God is crazy about me. I am not in bondage to the spirit of rejection. I receive the Spirit of adoption from the Holy Spirit. I have been adopted and I cry out, "Abba, Father." I belong in the Body of Christ and I have a unique place and purpose. The Lord will never forget or fail me.

Write out your personal declaration here.

Then declare it out loud.

_____

_____

_____

_____

_____

_____

_____

_____

_____

_____

_____

_____

_____

4. Willingly repent.

"And see if there is any grievous way in me." Psalm 139:24

We often can't control what others do to us, but we can choose our response. When we are rejected, our natural tendency is to fight, take flight, freeze, or fawn. We can agree with the rejection and believe those voices or reject the voices that counter the truth. We also can choose to not harden our hearts to those who have rejected us. If we harden our hearts and choose unforgiveness and bitterness, now we are sinning. This sin will keep us from flourishing and *FLOW*ing.

Who do you need to forgive as a result of rejection?

_____

_____

_____

_____

Allow God to search your heart for any area where repentance is needed. (Examples include people-pleasing, performance, insecurity, gossip, slander, pride, stubbornness, self-protection, control, etc.)

Repent of anything God shows you and pray for those who have persecuted you.

_____

_____

_____

_____

_____

Now, thank God for *FLOW*ing in that area of your heart. Receive His love and power to *FLOW*!

Chapter 6

Disarming Disappointment

"Those who look to Him are radiant, and their faces shall never be ashamed."

Psalm 34:5

Baby showers are my favorite! The excitement, anticipation, and beauty of a new mother is one of life's greatest joys. I attended a friend's baby shower recently and had the privilege of chatting with a beautiful young woman named Ava. We have crossed paths many times, but have not had the opportunity to enjoy any deep conversations.

I knew she had been married for about a decade and wanted to have children, so I boldly asked her if it was difficult to come to baby showers. In that moment, tears welled in Ava's beautiful greenish-brown eyes as her heart opened.

Ava always wears an authentic smile and beams with positivity. She is delightful, encouraging, and a giver to all who connect with her. My direct question brought to the surface what she was wrestling with and feeling deep beneath.

Not many weeks later, I ran into Ava at another friend's baby shower. She did not have to come, but she *chose* to come. Despite the torture of month-after-month negative pregnancy tests for seven years, Ava chose to celebrate her friend's pregnancy. Although Ava's heart was hurting from the delay of her own pregnancy, she still showed up to celebrate her friend. It has not been an easy journey for Ava.

After the sixth year of disappointment, Ava was at a women's event at church. She was so angry and hurt during worship that she walked out of the service. In the bathroom, she ran into a long-time friend and began to share some of her struggles. Her friend asked Ava a difficult question - Would God be enough for her to worship without a child? This question cut her to the core. She broke down sobbing, red-faced, and humbled right there in front of everyone. Ava's heart was devastated. She wrestled with thoughts like, "*What is God withholding from me? My husband deserves better. What is wrong with me?*"

Ava knows the cycle of disappointment, pain, then refocusing on God. She decided to order her thoughts to hope and trust that God has a much bigger plan at play. Infertility is heartbreaking. It can be refining and faith-testing, especially without a medical reason for the delay. Ava has chosen to allow her pain to push her to trust Jesus in a way she has never known. She knows nothing else in life can fulfill her but Him.

- No gift.

- No child.

- No husband.

- No job.

- No amount of money.

- Nothing can please the depth of her soul - *only Him*.

Yet, Ava wrestled in this agonizing battle of pain and disappointment month after month. Ava can choose to *bail on God* or *believe in God*. Believing in God through repetitive disappointment takes massive faith. Ava has chosen to believe in God's plan, trust His goodness towards her, and keep her heart alive in faith - even when it hurts. There is no doubt Ava is among the heroes of the faith. I am standing in agreement with Ava for her miracle child. Will you do the same? Will you stop and pray for Ava?

Ava's infertility journey reminds me of Hannah in the Bible. I feel close to Hannah. When I traveled to Israel years ago, I visited Shiloh, where Hannah dedicated her miracle child to the Lord. Visiting Shiloh was one of my favorite places in Israel and surprisingly captivated me the most. I felt like I was on holy ground. After the Israelites conquered the Promised Land, they divided it into twelve tribes. Shiloh was Israel's capital and tabernacle site for 369 years. The Ark of the Covenant rested inside the tabernacle and incense was offered to God day and night.

This holy place is where Hannah, *after her years of delay and disappointment*, brought her promised child to give to the Lord's service.

Let's stop now and read Hannah's story together.

Read 1 Samuel 1:2-2:21.

In Samuel 1:10, how did Hannah feel?

_____

_____

In verse 11, what did Hannah vow?

_____

_____

Hannah was in so much distress crying out to the Lord that Eli, the priest, thought she was drunk. What was Hannah's response in 1 Samuel 1:15?

_____

_____

Who saw Hannah's pain and opened her womb?

_____

_____

What did Hannah do with the miracle child?

_____

_____

Did Hannah have more children after Samuel?

_____

_____

Hannah labored over Samuel - *her miracle* - in prayer. Samuel, a prophet, played a significant role in transitioning from biblical judges to the Kingdom of Israel under Saul and David. David is the author of Psalm 139, which we are studying in this book. Samuel anointed David as king of Israel before his death.

Samuel was a poignant man of God in his time. He directed some of the most monumental transitions in biblical history. It makes me wonder if Hannah would have chosen to give Samuel to God if she didn't have to wait so long for him? It seems like Hannah's wait made her more willing to commit Samuel to God. What if your waiting is just as significant as Hannah's?

Like Hannah and Ava, when things don't come easily, I believe God has a master plan. I don't know what your disappointments are, but God sees and knows. It may not be infertility. It may be waiting on a spouse. Waiting for a job, to be healed, for real friends, or for the truth to come out. Whatever disappointments or delays you are experiencing, you can trust God has only good in store for you, my friend. Will you choose to believe He is good?

Let's filter the disappointments you are experiencing now.

1. Filter your thoughts and emotions.

What disappointment is the Holy Spirit bringing up right now? Write your first thoughts.

_____

_____

_____

_____

_____

What are some other areas where you have encountered disappointments in the past?

_____

_____

_____

_____

_____

What thoughts about disappointment circulate in your mind and emotions?

_____

_____

_____

_____

_____

What do you believe about yourself or God as a result of the disappointments you have faced?

_____

_____

_____

_____

_____

How are you acting and behaving as a result of the disappointments you have faced?

_____

_____

_____

_____

_____

2. Let God love you.

According to Psalm 139, what does God think about you?

_____

_____

_____

_____

_____

Look up Psalm 34:18. Where is God with the disappointment you are facing right now?

_____

_____

_____

_____

_____

Allow the Holy Spirit to speak truth to you personally now. Ask Him to tell you how much He loves you.

_____

_____

_____

_____

_____

3. Order your thoughts.

"As a man thinks in his heart, so he is." Proverbs 23:7

Use the following Scriptures to write your own personal declaration to order your thoughts to the truth and resist a spirit of despair and disappointment.

"To all who mourn in Israel, he will give a crown of beauty for ashes, a joyous blessing instead of mourning, festive praise instead of despair. In their righteousness, they will be like great oaks that the Lord has planted for his own glory." Isaiah 61:3 (NLT)

"How precious are your thoughts about me, O God. They cannot be numbered." Psalm 138:17 (NLT)

"We put our hope in the Lord. He is our help and our shield. In him our hearts rejoice, for we trust in his holy name. Let your unfailing love surround us, Lord, for our hope is in you alone." Psalm 33:20-22 (NLT)

"Always be full of joy in the Lord. I say it again - rejoice!" Philippians 4:4 (NLT)

"The Lord hears his people when they call to him for help. He rescues them from all their troubles." Psalm 34:17 (NLT)

"God will make this happen, for he who calls you is faithful." 1 Thessalonians 5:24 (NLT)

"Keep on asking, and you will receive what you ask for. Keep on seeking, and you will find. Keep on knocking, and the door will be opened to you. For everyone who asks, receives. Everyone who seeks finds. And to everyone who knocks, the door will be opened." Matthew 7:7-8 (NLT)

"The Lord kept his word and did for Sarah exactly what he had promised. She became pregnant, and she gave birth to a son for Abraham in his old age. This happened at just the time God had said it would." Genesis 21:1-2 (NLT)

"Blessed is she who has believed that the Lord would fulfill his promises to her!" Luke 1:45 (NIV)

"My flesh and heart may fail, but God is the strength of my heart and my portion forever." Psalm 73:26 (NIV)

"God is not a man, so he does not lie. He is not human, so he does not change his mind. Has he ever spoken and failed to act? Has he ever promised and not carried it through?" Numbers 23:19 (NLT)

Here is a declaration of truth when disappointment invades.

Even when my heart fails with disappointment, God is the strength of my heart. I trust you, Jesus, with the details of my life. I know that you are for me and your plans for me are good. You are faithful to all of your promises and your promises to me are "Yes" and "Amen." God will give me a crown of beauty for ashes, joy for mourning, and praise for despair. My heart rejoices in your unfailing love. My hope is in you alone, Lord. I will continue to ask you in prayer for what you have promised. I will continue to trust your ways and your timing in all things. Thank you for your faithfulness to me.

Use the space below to write your own declaration, then say it out loud.

_____

_____

_____

_____

_____

_____

_____

_____

_____

_____

_____

_____

4. Willingly repent.

"...*And see if there be any grievous way in me.*" Psalm 139:24

How do you need to regain trust in God again as a result of the disappointment you have faced?

_____

_____

_____

_____

_____

_____

Allow God to search your heart for any area where change is needed, and write it out below.

_____

_____

_____

_____

_____

_____

_____

Do you need to forgive anyone? Do you need to forgive yourself or even God? Write your thoughts below.

_____

_____

_____

_____

_____

_____

_____

Take some time to repent of anything God shows you in your heart and allow God to fill you with trust in Him and faith for the future.

_____

_____

_____

_____

_____

_____

_____

_____

_____

_____

Feel the release! Thank God for *FLOW*ing in faith now.

Chapter 7

Trading Injustice for Justice

"The Lord himself will fight for you. Just stay calm."

Exodus 14:14 (NLT)

We have all heard the saying, "Life is not fair." If we live long enough, we realize it is true to some extent in our own human experience. My son passed away on December 11 and my friend's son received his remission status on December 11. *Does that seem fair or just?* One of the attributes of God is justice: *"For the righteous Lord loves justice."* (Psalm 11:7) This is confusing to our human minds. Even in the circumstances that seem unjust to us, God is a just God, and His nature is rock-solid. There are some things we won't understand in this life, but one thing is sure: God is just and one day we will understand if we are believers in Jesus.

One April night changed everything for Cara. One decision. One moment. Life was normal...until it wasn't. Cara's son, Jason, was an exceptionally talented young man. He was in the gifted program from second grade through high school. He played the guitar, excelled in talented drama, and played football. His empathy, sense of humor, and smile would light up any room. By high school graduation, Jason had earned 23 college credit hours. He started his first year at a top state university.

Jason planned to come home from college the Saturday morning before spring break. So, he made plans to have a friend over the Friday night before. These friends were celebrating the end of a term and the beginning of a much-needed break. Sadly, that night, they turned from innocent fun to drug usage.

Jason's friend awakened to Cara calling him to find out when Jason would be home. It was then the friend found Jason unconscious. In fear, the friend abandoned Jason instead of calling for help. Jason's friend said he left before midnight. Later, it was revealed he stayed all night. He claimed he hadn't seen Jason since 11:30 p.m. the night before, because he was trying to avoid consequences for the drug use.

The friend ran in fear. He didn't call 911 to help his friend. After Cara's calls were ignored, her mother's intuition knew something wasn't right. She called the apartment complex manager and asked them to go see if he was alright. She also hopped in her car in a frantic, one-hour drive.

Cara arrived at Jason's apartment community, only to be met by a police officer. He notified her that Jason, her talented, handsome son, was deceased. Gone. It was obvious he was left alone for hours, unconscious and unattended.

Would Jason still be here today if only his friend had called for help? Today, I write Cara's story on Jason's actual birthday exactly six years later. I am sure Cara still wonders what his life would look like today. Would he be enjoying his career? Marrying the love of his life? Buying his first house? Instead, she is left with only memories. All the while, his friend is living a life with no consequences after leaving Jason alone to die. Can you imagine the anger, the rage, and the injustice? Cara had to decide what she would do with this injustice. How would she face the gambit of piercing emotions? She could hate and retaliate, or she could forgive and trust God with what she could not control.

She could not change her son's or his friend's choices that horrible night. She can only choose her choices now. Cara chose to respond well to this tortuous situation. Thankfully, Cara didn't crawl into a hole and hide. She turned her injustice to justice for others by helping pass a bill called *"Failure to Seek Assistance."* This bill holds someone accountable if they see a person in distress, unconscious, or dead without calling 911. Cara brought action to her injustice to prevent this type of scenario from happening to others. Cara eventually shifted her mind from her pain to her purpose.

I connected with this powerful woman just a few months ago at a group for women who have lost children. Cara lives filled with faith, encouragement, and hope for other mothers. She has been my co-pilot in this group and has learned how to process her pain healthily and lead others into healing too.

Cara still faces the anger and pain of losing her son. However, she learned how to *FLOW* in her heart and process her pain with God. She has decided to consistently forgive the friend who abandoned her son. She has also decided to consistently trust God with her loss. She encourages other mothers who are facing the devastation of injustice. When she encounters women who have lost children, she points them to the One who knows what it's like to lose a son - God, the Father. She has chosen to lead others and help them walk in forgiveness toward those who have mishandled their precious loved ones. Cara is a strong, faith-filled woman who looks to her Redeemer for help. She lives in the reality that heaven is our home as believers in Christ.

Cara and I will understand more when we meet Jesus face-to-face about the whys. Until then, we trust in the God with whom we have a personal relationship. We both know He is good and His love and goodness gives us hope for our futures.

When we look in the Bible, we see others who have experienced injustice, just like many of my friends who have lost children to tragic, unfair events and diseases. When I think of injustice, I can't help but to think of Hagar in the Bible. Hagar is introduced in Genesis 16. She is an Egyptian woman who was most likely one of the maidservants whom the king of Egypt bestowed upon Abram, among other gifts. (Genesis 12:16)

In Genesis 15, God made a covenant with Abram that his offspring would be like the "number of the stars" and Abram believed. Abram and Sarai must have waited many years before chapter 16 was written because they started scheming with their own plans.

Read Genesis chapter 16, then answer the following questions:

Whose idea was it to give Hagar to Abram as a wife? Who agreed?

_____

_____

Was any of this Hagar's idea? Did she have a choice?

_____

_____

After Hagar conceived, what problems arose?

_____

_____

Sarai dealt harshly with Hagar. What did Hagar do next?

_____

_____

Who found Hagar by a spring of water in the wilderness? What did the angel ask her?

_____

_____

What did the Lord do about Hagar's affliction? (v. 11)

_____

_____

What did Hagar call the name of the Lord? (v. 13)

_____

_____

Genesis 16:13-14 reads, "'*You are the God who sees me.*' *She also said, 'Have I truly seen the One who sees me?' So that well was named Beer-lahai-roi (which means "well of the Living One who sees me").*"

The Lord saw Hagar while running away in the desert and met her there. She found herself in uncontrollable circumstances that made her feel like a victim, still the Lord met her as "the God of seeing." He saw Hagar in her distress. He saw her and strengthened her.

The Lord met my friend Cara in her unjust desert. He sees all the injustices you have faced too. People may have appeared to get away with injustice, but He is the God who sees, and He is our just vindicator in all circumstances.

Filter the responses to the injustices you have experienced now.

1. Filter your thoughts and emotions.

What injustice is the Holy Spirit bringing up right now?

_____

_____

_____

What are some other areas and situations in which you have encountered injustice?

_____

_____

_____

What thoughts about this injustice are circulating in your mind and emotions?

_____

_____

_____

What do you believe about yourself as a result of the injustice?

_____

_____

_____

How are you acting and behaving as a result of the injustice?

_____

_____

_____

2. Let God love you.

What does God think about you? Refer to Psalm 139 and Genesis 16:13-14 while you answer.

_____

_____

_____

According to Proverbs 17:15, where is God with the injustice you are facing right now?

_____

_____

_____

Allow the Holy Spirit to speak to you personally now. Ask Him to tell you how much He loves you.

_____

_____

_____

_____

_____

_____

_____

Now declare this paraphrase from Psalm 139 aloud.

I can never escape your presence and love! Whether I go to high places or low places, your love will pursue me. Even when I go to dark places, you will follow me and bring me to the light. You formed the uniqueness of my personality, mind, and body. I am wonderfully created just as you intended. Nothing about me is a mistake. Thank you for making me wonderfully complex!

You wove me together perfectly how you liked. I like what you created and accept who I am completely. Your thoughts toward me are precious and too many to count. Every morning when I wake up you are there, no matter how I feel. You look at me and are proud of who I am. I am loved today and every day by You!

3. Order your thoughts.

"As a man thinks in his heart, so he is." Proverbs 23:7

Use the following Scriptures to write your own personal declaration to order your thoughts to the truth and resist a spirit of victimization.

"Beloved, never avenge yourselves, but leave it to the wrath of God, for it is written, "Vengeance is mine, I will repay, says the Lord. Feed your hungry enemy; give him a drink. This will heap burning coals." Romans 12:19-20

"He who justifies the wicked and he who condemns the righteous are both like an abomination to the Lord." Proverbs 17:15

"There are six things that the Lord hates, seven that are an abomination to him: haughty eyes, a lying tongue, and hands that shed innocent blood, a heart that devises wicked plans, feet that make haste to run to evil, a false witness who breathes out lies, and one who sows discord among brothers." Proverbs 6:16-19

"But I say to you who hear, Love your enemies, do good to those who hate you, bless those who curse you, pray for those who abuse you." Luke 6:27-28

"Do not be overcome by evil, but overcome evil with good." Romans 12:21

Here is an example of a declaration:

The Lord sees me. The Lord sees the truth of what has happened to me and what was done to me. God is Jehovah - Tsidkenu. He is the Lord who makes all things right in His time and in His way. I may not see how He does it now, but He will handle the situation if I release it to Him completely. I trust God. I trust that He will defend me. The Lord said, "Vengeance is mine, and He will repay." My job is to bless those who curse me and to pray for those who mistreat me. I am not a victim in Christ. The Lord makes me victorious, and He will handle every unjust act toward me because He hates a false witness, and injustice is an abomination to Him. As I release my offenders, the Lord will free me and make all things right.

Write your personal declaration here, then say it out loud.

_____

_____

_____

_____

_____

_____

_____

_____

4. Willingly repent.

We can't control what others do to us, but we can choose our response. We also can choose to release to God those who have been unjust to us. If we harden our hearts and choose unforgiveness and bitterness, now we are sinning. This sin will keep us from flourishing and FLOWing.

I know, it's counterintuitive to repent when we or our loved one has been victimized. Ask the Lord to help you release and forgive the perpetrators so that God can take it from here. I know it is difficult. You are not saying it is right, but you are releasing control from yourself to God, which is the ultimate judge. He will take it and make it right because he is our God of righteousness.

What unforgiveness do you need to repent of right now as a result of injustice?

_____

_____

_____

_____

_____

Allow God to search your heart for any area where repentance is needed (Examples include control, rage, anger, getting even, victimization, and apathy).

Repent of anything God shows you and experience the release!

Chapter 8

Finding Grace in Grief

"Sometimes you have to let go of the picture of what you thought it would be like and learn to find joy in the story you are actually living."

Anonymous

Losing a child is unthinkable. When we lost our first-born son, Joseph, to brain cancer at four years old, it felt sur-real. The waves of sadness would punch me in the gut out of nowhere. When trying to accept a new-normal, I didn't want to. I wanted my old life again. How would I find a new joyous life again?

My faith was tested. Did I believe our life's purpose is to know God, follow Him, then go to eternity to be with Je-sus? I had to remind myself that I did my job with Joseph. He knew God. There was purpose in his life - he brought others to

Jesus, then he had the privilege to go ahead of us to spend eternity with Him. Joseph's last spoken words to us was, *"Do you know Jesus?"*

Although I didn't understand why Joseph passed away so young after praying and believing for a miracle, I made the choice to trust God. I trusted God was good instead of taking the bait to blame Him and harden my heart because I didn't get what I expected. I got through the loss of Joseph because I trusted God's nature - He is good even though I lost my son. I was able to trust God because I knew Him.

My friend, Ellen, experienced a different kind of loss after losing the 40-year love of her life to cancer as well. Ellen was married to her soulmate, best friend, lover, and protector. He was not a perfect man, but he was the perfect man for her. Ellen's marriage was a place of fulfillment, joy, and purpose. Then, after a seven-year battle with cancer, her husband's war was over, and the most difficult fight of her life began.

She had joked with her husband about hiding under the covers if he died first. Life without him was unbearable. After being forced to contend with her worst fear, Ellen stood face-to-face with a big decision to make. Would she stay "under the covers" or would she re-imagine a life without her husband? Could life be fulfilling again?

As a Christ follower, Ellen knew staying stuck was not an option for her. Since she had decided to follow Jesus decades prior, her goal was always to glorify Him through her life, even when her life did not turn out as she expected. Ellen lived to be an example of God's goodness, grace, and mercy.

Now, she had an intentional choice to make. Would the pain of her loss defeat her, or would the pain propel her to a new purpose?

Before Ellen became a widow, the only widow she knew was her mother-in-law who had died one year prior. She had no contemporaries who had lost their spouse. She had supportive friends, pastors, and family members. She felt adrift and even helpless while navigating grief.

No one could comprehend the depth of pain Ellen felt, or so it seemed. She read everything she could get her hands on about loss, grief, and widowhood. She began to understand what she was feeling was normal, but in no way did it feel normal to her. Once, she heard a man share about the death of his spouse who said it felt like someone had taken a chainsaw to him and had cut him in half without anesthesia. This was a statement Ellen could understand. Now, she needed to figure out what to do with the half that remained.

Ellen's strong faith in Jesus helped her to trust God's Word as truth above her emotions. Her emotions felt one way, but God's Word was the truth she chose to follow. Ellen embraced Romans 5:1-5 which says,

"Therefore, having been justified by faith, we have peace with God through our Lord Jesus Christ, through whom also we have access by faith into this grace in which we stand, and rejoice in hope of the glory of God. And not only that, but we also glory in tribulations, knowing tribulation produces perseverance; and perseverance, character; and character hope. Now hope does not disappoint because the love of God has been poured out in our hearts by the Holy Spirit who was given to us."

Ellen was in deep grief and pain, yet she clung to the Word of God and trusted it more than her emotions. As she looked back, she could see how God made what seemed impossible possible.

Ellen leaned on God's Word to overcome grief, fear, and even panic. She trusted His truths. Trusting takes tremendous faith when our flesh is screaming in pain. Words like "peace, joy, and hope" are woven throughout Scripture. Her feelings could not be based on emotions but on God's truths. Ellen chose to truly believe the Scriptures more than her own thoughts and feelings. She made a decision that this pain would not drag her under, but she would allow God to use her pain for His purpose.

Her pain allowed her a platform to share hope with others. Since this time, Ellen has encouraged and ministered to many widows who have lost husbands. She has encouraged them and walked alongside them in her small group each week. Ellen still experiences times of sadness. She still misses her husband often, but the "joy of the Lord is her strength." (Nehemiah 8:10) Now she is able to take her "half" and live a life of joy.

The Bible portrays for us a trio of widows who are forced to decide their next steps and *FLOW* again, like Ellen. Three women named Naomi, Ruth, and Orpah found themselves to be widows simultaneously. Naomi was Ruth and Orpah's mother-in-law. Imagine Naomi's losses. She lost her husband and both of her sons *at the same time.*

Naomi and her husband, Elimelech, left the land of Judah due to a famine. They went searching for food in the nearby land of Moab and settled there. Their sons grew up and married Moabite women. For reasons we don't know, all three husbands died. After their passing, Naomi heard her homeland's famine ended. There was food in Judah now. She decided to go home and urged her daughters-in-law to stay in their homeland and to return to their families.

Read Ruth 1:9-10.

What was their response to Naomi's news of leaving Moab?

_____

_____

_____

Read Ruth 1:14.

After Naomi urged them to go home again, what did they do?

_____

_____

_____

One daughter-in-law stayed in Moab with her family. The other clung to Naomi and the Hebrew God for an unknown future. One person stayed loyal to her pagan gods. Another followed Naomi's God with love and devotion.

What did Ruth say in Ruth 1:16-17?

_____

_____

_____

Ruth was determined to follow Naomi's God. She left everything to embrace Him and His possibilities. Ruth explored new territory after losing her husband. She followed her new-found God. Her love for Him gave her the courage to press on into the unknown.

Read Ruth 2.

What did Ruth find in verse 13?

_____

_____

_____

_____

Read Ruth 3.

What plan did Naomi devise?

_____

_____

_____

_____

Read Ruth 4.

How did Ruth find a new life in Judah?

_____

_____

_____

_____

Read Ruth 4:18-22.

In whose lineage were Ruth's descendants?

_____

_____

_____

_____

Ruth's courage to cling to faith in her loss and pain positioned her to be in God's plan and purpose for her life and even the redemption of humanity. Ellen, like Ruth and Naomi, made a choice towards God's plan and purpose. Their choice to move forward gives hope and redemption to her life and also to the lives of others.

What about you? Have you decided what to do with the "half" or "piece" of what is left of your loss? Maybe you have not lost a husband, but you lost something else.

- A dream

- A parent

- A child

- Your reputation

- A future

- Money

- A home

- Your innocence

- Your peace

- Your health

Jesus is gentle, kind, patient, and good. I promise He has a plan for your life - even in the midst of the deep losses you have encountered. I don't know what you have lost, but this is what I do know - He will restore your heart and life and fill you with hope for the future. According to Romans 8, God has a way of turning all things around to work together for good no matter the loss. What a hope! Even the assignments of the enemy can be turned around and worked together for our good for all who trust in Jesus.

Grief is a process. God is gracious and loving in the process. The process takes time, and it differs for everyone. I knew this all too well due to the death of my son.

There comes a time though when we all must choose whether our pain or our purpose will define the rest of our lives. May the Holy Spirit guide you as you filter the pain and perhaps your loss of trust in Him from the events you have encountered in your life.

1. Filter your thoughts and emotions.

What pain or belief from loss is the Holy Spirit bringing up right now? Write your first thought.

_____

_____

_____

_____

_____

What are some other areas where you have experienced loss, pain, and grief?

_____

_____

_____

_____

_____

_____

What thoughts about the losses are circulating in your mind and emotions?

_____

_____

_____

_____

_____

What do you believe about yourself or God as a result of the loss and pain?

_____

_____

_____

_____

_____

How are you acting and behaving as a result of the losses in your life?

_____

_____

_____

_____

_____

2. Let God love you.

What does God think about you? (Psalm 139)

_____

_____

_____

_____

_____

According to Psalm 34:18, where is God with the loss you are facing right now?"

_____

_____

_____

_____

_____

_____

Allow the Holy Spirit to speak to you personally now. Ask Him to tell you how much he loves you.

_____

_____

_____

_____

_____

_____

_____

_____

_____

_____

3. Order your thoughts.

"*As a man thinks in his heart, so he is.*" Proverbs 23:7

Use the Scriptures below to write your own declaration.

"*The Lord is near to those who have a broken heart, and saves such as have a contrite spirit.*" Psalm 34:18 (CEV)

"My soul melts from heaviness; strengthen me according to your word." Psalm 119:28 (CEV)

"You number my wanderings; put tears into Your bottle; are they not in Your book?" Psalm 56:8 (CEV)

"He is despised and rejected by men, a Man of sorrows and acquainted with grief. And we hid, as it were, our faces from Him; He was despised, and we did not esteem Him." Isaiah 53:3 (NASB)

"Who shall separate us from the love of Christ? Shall tribulation, or distress, or persecution, or famine, or nakedness, or peril, or sword?" Romans 8:35 (NKJV)

"Be anxious for nothing, but in everything by prayer and supplication, with thanksgiving, let your requests be made known to God; and the peace of God, which surpasses all understanding, will guard your hearts and minds through Christ Jesus." Philippians 4:6-7 (CEV)

"Yea, though I walk through the valley of the shadow of death, I will fear no evil; for you are with me; Your rod and your staff, they comfort me." Psalm 23:4 (NKJV)

"And He said to me, 'My grace is sufficient for you, for My strength is made perfect in weakness.'" 2 Corinthians 12:9 (NKJV)

"If you are tired from carrying heavy burdens, come to me and I will give you rest. Take the yoke I give you. Put it on your shoulders and learn from me. I am gentle and humble and you will find rest." Matthew 11:28-29 (CEV)

"While we do not look at the things which are seen, but at the things which are not seen. For the things which are seen are temporary, but the things which are not seen are eternal." 2 Corinthians 4:18 (NKJV)

A declaration of truth when grief is overwhelming

I am a child of God. I am never alone, forsaken, or abandoned. God is for me and the Holy Spirit is with me right now. In His presence is fullness of joy. God is my comfort and strength. The Lord will renew my strength and give me courage for today and tomorrow. Jesus is acquainted with all my grief. He was a man of sorrows, and I cast my sorrow upon Him. He is carrying my sorrow, pain, and grief from loss. He is with me and will lift the pain from me. I will not sink, but I will be lifted. God's righteous right hand holds my heart and life. He will show me my next steps and will comfort me today. May the Holy Spirit fill me right now with love, peace, comfort, and joy in His presence. I am more than a conqueror in Christ Jesus.

Now, write your own declaration, then declare it aloud.

_____

_____

_____

_____

_____

_____

4. Willingly repent.

> *"And see if there is any grievous way in me."* Psalm 139:24

How do you need to regain trust in God again as a result of the loss you have faced?

_____

_____

_____

_____

_____

Allow God to search your heart for any area where change is needed. Who do you need to forgive? Where do you need to forgive yourself or even God?

_____

_____

_____

_____

_____

_____

Take time now to repent of anything God shows you in your heart and allow God to fill you with trust in Him and faith for the future.

_____

_____

_____

_____

_____

_____

_____

_____

_____

_____

Thank God you are *FLOW*ing in faith now.

Chapter 9

Releasing Resentment

"The worst resentment that anybody can have is one you feel justified to keep."[7]

Louis Gossett, Jr.

Maria had it all. She had the perfect family. Maria vacationed several times a year, and everything had its place. She met her amazing husband when she was young. They both came from strong families. Maria exuded positivity and happiness. There was always something exciting going on with Maria. If one word could describe her life, it would be blessed.

Life was moving along beautifully until Maria hit her forties. She began grappling with mounting frustration, particularly around the holidays with her extended family. These frustrations were often minimized as no big deal. After all, she was so blessed she did not feel it was right to focus on these seemingly small things that bothered her.

Maria's people-pleasing personality did not want to rock the boat. Year after year, she wrestled with her feelings of frustration around the holidays. When she brought the extended family situation up to her husband, he would routinely make light of it. He did not realize how much the frustrations were gnawing at Maria. She continued pressing through the frustration for years. She thought that glossing over her pain was the right thing to do because she was a Christian. Maria continued people-pleasing because, ultimately, she did not want to be rejected.

Maria finally realized she was not okay. She decided to go to counseling. Something toxic had crept up in her life. She was angry and it was erupting out like a volcano in multiple ways. The counselor told Maria she was resentful toward her husband. The lightbulb came on. Her husband was amazing and kind. How could she have a problem with him? She had no idea. The resentment kept growing and growing until she had lost positive feelings toward him. She didn't know why.

Within 24 hours Maria was able to meet with her husband and let her pain and resentment all out. She communicated all the ways the people-pleasing for the extended family caused resentment over time. Her heart was clogged toward him because she felt he did not take her feelings seriously. Once the root issue was revealed, she was able to express it. Her husband apologized. They both were able to communicate what they needed and extended forgiveness to each other. Immediately, Maria's positive feelings toward her husband returned. The *FLOW* was opened! It was truly miraculous how quickly things changed.

I can't help but to think how many relationships have ended up miserable or dissolved completely due to unattended and displaced resentment. Maria did not pinpoint her resentment toward her husband immediately. She was aware of the disconnection, frustration, and lack of positive feelings toward him. But she didn't know why. She was starting to believe untruths about him and her internal case was building bigger and stronger. Thankfully, Maria got to the root instead of continuing in the same toxic direction.

I can relate to Maria. I had resentment toward my husband as well, but I knew it. It's bad when you have resentment, you know it, and feel entitled to it. Ouch, that was hard to say! I wrestled with resentment instead of communicating in a positive way and trusting God. For years, I didn't know how to communicate my frustration proactively. I did not have the skills, so I became passive-aggressive. I would absorb and over-give until I snapped.

I became pregnant with our first son, Joseph, six months after marriage, resigned from my job, and stayed home with the children. I yielded my personal ambitions and life balance for this season, while I felt like my husband kept his life balance intact. I felt like I was giving so much more than him. I became resentful. Instead of being self-aware, properly communicating my needs, and coming together to find a life balance that worked for both of us, our lack of healthy communication skills drove a wedge. I didn't know how to properly communicate my needs. This made my husband defensive. Therefore, he dismissed and often invalidated my complaints out of his own insecurity.

If I would have communicated better and he would have affirmed and validated my feelings better, we would have experienced much more peace and unity. The truth is, I was making major sacrifices for the well-being of our family. We were making the best choices for our family together. It was still hard though, especially for me. He learned to validate and praise the sacrifice I was making. I learned how to calmly communicate what I needed before I became passive-aggressive.

Jon is my greatest supporter in the work of ministry God has called me to do and the dreams God has given me to accomplish. I just wish we would have learned this sooner. It would have saved so much pain and strife as we were working against each other. I am grateful that now we can help other young couples communicate better to address rising resentment instead of dealing with it later like Maria and me.

Resentment is an unforgiving spirit that starts and ends when one feels misunderstood when someone forgets to acknowledge how much one has sacrificed for them. It occurs when one expects so much more from others because they would have been willing to do much more for them. Resentment can easily sneak up on all of us in a variety of ways. It can stifle our hearts.

Resentment goes back to the first family in Genesis 4. Here Cain resented his brother, Abel, for giving a wholehearted offering to God while Cain gave a half-hearted offering. God accepted Abel's whole-hearted offering, but rejected Cain's half-heartedness. Cain resented Abel and then killed him in his anger. *How many times do we kill relationships due to resentment and anger?*

Let's read this encounter together. Read Genesis 4:1-16.

What stood out to you?

_____

_____

_____

_____

Resentment can build when you feel like you are unfairly treated. What should Cain have done instead of killing his brother? Did his brother do anything wrong? What should Cain have done after he killed his brother? Read Genesis 4:6-7, and 9.

_____

_____

_____

_____

What should we do when we feel resentment creeping in?

_____

_____

_____

_____

1. Filter your thoughts and emotions.

What resentment is the Holy Spirit bringing up right now? Write your first thoughts.

_____

_____

_____

_____

What are some other areas and situations where you have embraced resentment?

_____

_____

_____

_____

What thoughts about this resentment are circulating in your mind and emotions?

_____

_____

_____

_____

What are you believing about yourself as a result of the resentment you have?

_____

_____

_____

_____

How are you acting and behaving as a result of the resentment you have?

_____

_____

_____

_____

2. Let God love you.

What does God think about you? (Go to Psalm 139 again.)

_____

_____

_____

_____

Where is God with the resentment you are facing right now?

_____

_____

_____

_____

Allow the Holy Spirit to speak truth to you personally now. Ask Him to tell you how much He loves you.

_____

_____

_____

_____

Now declare this paraphrase from Psalm 139 aloud:

I can never escape your presence and love! Whether I go to high places or low places, your love will pursue me. Even when I go to dark places, you will follow me and bring me to the light. You formed the uniqueness of my personality, mind, and body. I am wonderfully created just as you intended. Nothing about me is a mistake. Thank you for making me wonderfully complex! You wove me together perfectly how you liked. I like what you created and accept who I am completely. Your thoughts toward me are precious and too many to count. Every morning when I wake up *you are there, no matter how I feel. You look at me and are proud of who I am. I am loved today and every day by You!*

3. Order your thoughts.

"As a man thinks in his heart, so he is." Proverbs 23:7

Use the following Scriptures to write your personal declaration to reject resentment.

"Whoever loves his brother abides in the light, and in him there is no cause for stumbling. But whoever hates his brother is in the darkness and walks in the darkness, and does not know where he is going because the darkness has blinded his eyes." 1 John 2:11

"And whenever you stand praying, forgive, if you have anything against anyone, so that your Father also who is in heaven may forgive you your trespasses." Mark 11:25

"Judge not, and you will not be judged; condemn not, and you will not be condemned; forgive, and you will be forgiven." Luke 6:37

"See to it that no one fails to obtain the grace of God; that no 'root of bitterness' springs up and causes trouble, and by it many become defiled." Hebrews 12:15

"Let all bitterness and wrath and anger and clamor and slander be put away from you, along with all malice." Ephesians 4:31

"Love is patient and kind; love does not envy or boast; it is not arrogant or rude. It does not insist on its own way; it is not irritable or resentful." 1 Corinthians 13:4-7

"Then Peter came up and said to him, 'Lord, how often will my brother sin against me, and I forgive him? As many as seven times?' Jesus said to him, 'I do not say to you seven times, but seventy-times-seven.'" Matthew 18:21-22

A declaration to resist resentment

I recognize resentment is the beginning stages of bitterness so I take it to the cross now. When my brother or sister sins against me, I will forgive as often as needed. I give my resentment building toward (   ) now. I will communicate in a loving way the frustration I am experiencing to all involved then release it to you. I will not be the judge of (   ). You are the only judge. I am a forgiving person. I choose to believe the best in my family, friends, and neighbors. I can be forgiving and also have a boundary to protect myself from others' poor behavior at the same time. I am full of grace and truth.

Write your own declaration here:

_____

_____

_____

_____

_____

_____

_____

_____

_____

_____

_____

_____

_____

_____

_____

_____

_____

_____

4. Willingly repent.

"And see if there be any grievous way in me." Psalm 139:24

We can't control what others do to us, but we can choose our response. When we are rejected our natural tendency is to fight, flight, freeze, or fawn. We can either agree with the rejection and believe the voices spoken in the rejection, or we can reject the voices that counter the truth of who we are in Christ.

We don't have to harden our hearts toward those who have rejected us. If we harden our hearts and choose unforgiveness and bitterness, now we are sinning. This sin will keep us from flourishing and *FLOW*ing. We can choose to give that resentment to God and make an exchange.

I know, it's counterintuitive when we are truly the victim in a situation. It is possible to exchange our resentment, put it in God's hands, and receive His love and grace. Your heavenly Father can be trusted and will take care of it better than you can.

Where is the resentment building in you right now?

_____

_____

_____

_____

Allow God to search your heart for any area where repentance is needed.

_____

_____

_____

_____

Repent of anything God shows you and pray for those who have persecuted you. Feel the release!

_____

_____

_____

_____

Now thank God for *FLOW*ing in that area of your heart. Receive His comfort, love, and power!

_____

_____

_____

_____

Chapter 10

Bounding Beyond Betrayal

*"Let me be on my guard when the world puts on a loving face, for it will,
if possible, betray me as it did my master, with a kiss."*[8]

Charles Spurgeon

Lauren and Chris fell in love at eighteen years old. They were two young people who were figuring out who they were while simultaneously growing up together. They knew the Lord drew them together and they wanted to do great things with Him and for Him. Their future together looked bright.

Fast forward 20 years and everything was different. Chris did not believe in God or his marriage to Lauren anymore. If he didn't believe in God, how could he believe in covenant marriage originated by God? Lauren was feeling the distance and was in shock when he verbalized this to her.

She felt this was an attack on her family. She started to pray and have faith for the both of them for a miracle turnaround.

They went to counseling. It seemed only to make matters worse. They only touched on the symptoms and were not getting to the deep roots of hurt in Chris' childhood. Somewhere along the way, the rejection made Chris believe he wasn't good enough for Lauren. Insecurity and isolation kept them away from relationships with other healthy couples. The enemy lied to him. Offense came into his heart and locked him into a prison from which only forgiveness could release him.

Lauren had issues of her own. She was a people-pleaser. Lauren did not know how to communicate her feelings when her needs were not met. She did not want to be a burden on anyone, especially Chris. Lauren also privately battled with a fear of losing her life and leaving her children motherless. This fear grew into anxiety and paralyzed her.

Anxiety certainly had an affect on her marriage. She shoved her feelings down. The demands of life pushed Chris and Lauren into opposite directions. The locked-up places in their hearts kept them apart and drifting. The grueling grind of life, the whispers from the enemy, and the hurts and offenses from others all combined explosively. Lauren and Chris didn't know what to do with each other. Financially, they could not separate. There was intense frustration, yet they did not want their children to face the pain of divorce.

Early in this battle, the Lord asked Lauren if she would trust Him no matter the outcome. God asked Lauren if she would follow Him no matter what Chris chose. She can remember lying across her bed with tears streaming, looking at their wedding photos on the wall and gently hearing the Holy Spirit say, "*Follow Me.*" She didn't know the outcome.

She had to decide that her hope would be in Jesus above her preferred outcome. Lauren knew that true hope in Jesus is not about trusting in a specific outcome but in a bright future because Jesus is present. Lauren's dilemma was not whether she would follow Jesus, but whether she would place her trust in Him and not just what she wanted Him to do. Some days, she was full of hope and confidence. Other days, it was all she could do to pray the words, "Help my unbelief."

The first thing the Lord told Lauren to do was to trust and follow Him. The second thing he told her was to love Chris in a way that honored the Lord and was an example to her children. She did not always want to do this, especially when she was overlooked and neglected. Their marriage grew into a platonic relationship as Chris pulled further away. He was never abusive or violent, which is one of the reasons she stayed. I don't think anyone should endure physical abuse or expose their children violence. For Lauren, there was no romance, connection, or intimacy. They worked together to keep their home running. Every year, their anniversary came and went acknowledged only by the tear stains on Lauren's pillow. She lived like this for seven years while praying to God for a miracle.

Then one day, an unthinkable event happened. After becoming financially stronger, Chris decided to move out. Telling her children was the hardest thing she had ever done. Angry and helpless, her heart was clouded. When Chris moved out, Lauren didn't fall apart like she anticipated. She had already made the commitment to follow Jesus. He was even healing and sustaining her. Lauren also has no regrets in how she loved Chris, even when he didn't deserve love. She knew deep in her heart the Lord was honoring her obedience to Him in the respect and love she gave Chris.

People have often asked Lauren why she stayed so long. For her, it was never about staying or leaving, but guarding her heart and obeying the Lord. She knew she had to keep her eyes fixed on the Lord or she would sink, just like Peter out on the stormy water. (Matthew 14:29) Lauren had been in a brutal storm. She learned to guard her heart and not let bitterness take root. She fought to keep her heart *FLOW*ing. This was the biggest fight of all. Lauren could have let bitterness, betrayal, and abandonment reign over her. But that is not the Lord's will for her. She says, "I am called to be His daughter, and I am an overcomer!"

Lauren still does not know what the future holds. She still grips hope for a complete restoration in her marriage. She still prays for Chris and the restoration of his faith in Jesus. She also knows the Lord is holding her hand as she makes the choice each day to allow Jesus to be the center of her focus rather than what has happened to her marriage.

Lauren has contended for her heart. She has decided on the One she will follow and focus on. She knows the love of her God will never leave her or fail her. I am excited to witness this next season in Lauren's life. I know there will be redemption and healing. I know she will follow God and His purposes for her. Her best days are ahead because she has fought for her heart and stayed close to the Keeper of her heart.

In the Bible, there is a woman who reminds me of Lauren. Her name is Abigail. Abigail did not experience betrayal in the same way Lauren did. Yet, she modeled being a wife of honor. She lived with honor even when her husband was acting foolishly and indirectly betraying her by choosing himself over her well-being. Abigail was a faithful woman who continued to bless her husband and defend her home even when her foolish husband was tearing it down. In 1 Samuel 25, we learn Abigail was discerning and beautiful, but her husband, Nabal, was harsh and badly behaved.

David was hiding in the wilderness from Saul and saw that Nabal had plenty of sheep. David and his men had surrounded Nabal's estate and even protected Nabal's property. David sent ten of his men to politely greet Nabal, give a blessing of peace, and request an offering for an upcoming feast day.

Nabal responded selfishly and foolishly. (1 Samuel 25:11-12) This reply enraged David after all he had done to protect Nabal's estate. David rashly sent 400 men with swords in hand to destroy Nabal's entire household.

One of the young men told Abigail about her husband's foolish response and how David and his men were coming to destroy her household. Abigail quickly came up with a wise plan to intervene. She met David on the road with gifts and in humility threw herself on the ground to change David's mind. David listened to Abigail.

Abigail's character, intelligence, and response saved her life and the life of her children from her husband's foolish behavior. She even respected her husband despite his behavior.

Let's look at the wisdom and character of Abigail.

Read 1 Samuel 25:18-34.

What did Abigail do? How did she display intelligence, discernment, and honor?

_____

_____

_____

_____

Who was Abigail trying to save by stopping David?

_____

_____

_____

_____

What are some of the character traits you see in Abigail?

_____

_____

_____

_____

Read 1 Samuel 25:36-38.

What was Nabal doing while she was out saving his livelihood?

_____

_____

_____

_____

What did Abigail endure every day before this encounter with David's men?

_____

_____

_____

How did Abigail's story end?

_____

_____

_____

_____

How did Abigail and Lauren honor the Lord and protect their households even in undesirable circumstances with their husbands?

_____

_____

_____

_____

1. Filter your thoughts and emotions.

What pain or belief from betrayal is the Holy Spirit bringing up right now? Write your first thought.

_____

_____

_____

_____

What are some other areas where you have experienced betrayal in your life?

(Think: parent, spouse, friend, relative, boss, co-worker, etc.)

_____

_____

_____

_____

What betrayals circulate in your mind and emotions?

_____

_____

_____

_____

_____

What do you believe about yourself or God as a result of the betrayal you faced?

_____

_____

_____

_____

_____

How are you acting and behaving as a result of the betrayal?

_____

_____

_____

_____

_____

2. Let God love you.

What does God think about you? (Refer to Psalm 139)

_____

_____

_____

_____

_____

Where is God in the betrayal you are facing right now, according to Psalm 34:18?

_____

_____

_____

_____

_____

Allow the Holy Spirit to speak to you personally now. Ask Him to reveal to you how much he loves you and desires to defend you in this betrayal.

_____

_____

_____

_____

3. Order your thoughts.

"*As a man thinks in his heart, so he is.*" Proverbs 23:7

Use the following Scriptures to write a declaration to order your thinking about the betrayal in your life.

"*Evening and morning and at noon I utter my complaint and moan, and he hears my voice. He redeems my soul in safety from the battle that I wage, for many are arrayed against me. God will give ear and humble them, he who is enthroned from of old, because they do not change and do not fear God.*" Psalm 55:17-19

"*For my father and my mother have forsaken me, but the Lord will take me in.*" Psalm 27:10

"My companion stretched out his hand against his friends; he violated his covenant. His speech was smooth as butter, yet war was in his heart; his words were softer than oil, yet they were drawn swords. Cast your burden on the Lord, and he will sustain you; he will never permit the righteous to be moved." Psalm 55:20

"My flesh and my heart may fail, but God is the strength of my heart and my portion forever." Psalm 73:26

"Arise, O Lord, in your anger; lift yourself up against the fury of my enemies; awake for me; you have appointed a judgment." Psalm 7:6

"Do not repay evil for evil or reviling for reviling, but on the contrary, bless, for to this you were called, that you may obtain a blessing." 1 Peter 3:9

"A false witness will not go unpunished, and he who breathes out lies will perish." Proverbs 19:9

"A lying tongue hates its victims, and a flattering mouth works ruin." Proverbs 26:28

"Be merciful to me, O God, be merciful to me, for in you my soul takes refuge; in the shadow of your wings I will take refuge, till the storms of destruction pass by. I cry out to God Most High, to God who fulfills his purpose for me. He will send from heaven and save me; he will put to shame him who tramples on me. God will send out his steadfast love and his faithfulness!" Psalm 57:1-3

A declaration when betrayed

Father, you are my vindicator! You are the One who judges those who have betrayed me. I release the betrayal to You and You will deal with those who have dealt wrongly to me and my family. It is not my job to be the judge. That is Your job. My job is to forgive those who have wronged me and to trust You. You said if I cast my burden on You, You will sustain me, and You will not allow the righteous to be moved. I choose to respond with a blessing instead of repaying evil for evil. Even when my heart fails me, You are the strength of my heart. I will not be overtaken with You as my portion forever.

Write your own declaration here:

_____

_____

_____

_____

_____

_____

_____

_____

4. Willingly repent.

"And see if there be any grievous way in me." Psalm 139:24

How can you strengthen your trust in God again as a result of the betrayal?

_____

_____

_____

Allow God to search your heart for any area where change is needed. Do you need to forgive anyone? Do you need to forgive yourself or even God?

_____

_____

_____

Take some time to repent of anything God reveals where you have wanted revenge or control. Allow God to fill you with trust in Him and faith for the future.

_____

_____

_____

_____

_____

_____

_____

_____

Feel the burden released from you and placed on God.

Chapter 11

FLOW: Free to Love Others Well

"A new commandment I give to you, that you love one another: just as I have loved you, you also are to love one another."

John 13:34 (NLT)

Love is such a commonly used word. We say things like, "I love your outfit," or " I love ice cream." We toss out that word casually so when someone tells us they love us, it does not mean as much as it once did. In reality, a person does not feel our love by mere words. People feel loved by actions, presence, and consistency. Consistent positive interactions show people we love them.

Childhood trauma, unmet needs, angry responses, and relational inconsistency contribute to people being skeptical of others. How many times can a person tell someone he or she loves them, then is neglectful, harsh, or abandons them completely? These people grow into adults who have found love to be undependable. When we are inhibited by things like resentment, rejection, disappointment, betrayal, loss, and injustice, it's difficult to extend consistent love to others.

How can we fully love others when our hearts have lost their *FLOW*?

As we learn the skill of filtering our hearts and keeping our hearts in tune with God, we can love others better. It is only by experiencing God's love that we can truly love. We can't love in our own strength out of human effort alone. When we accept Christ as our Lord, He saves our soul. He also changes us from the inside out. We flow from a supernatural place of God's Kingdom. We can experience a love that is richly satisfying and tangible. We can experience this radiant love.

Remember, He created us to walk with Him in a garden of love and care. He longs to know us. He longs to generously pour out His love. All we must learn to do is to believe Him and receive His love. I pray you will learn to receive God's love by working through the processing guide in these pages and it becomes a consistent practice in your life. When we know and experience His love, we can trust Him. His love is dependable and steady. When we enjoy the safety of His love, we can endure the pains and rejections of this world and extend His love to others.

Some people around us do not know how to love because they have not connected with the real Source of love, who is Jesus. God demonstrated His love for us with the gift of His Son, so we might know the truth of His love and the hope of His plan. Yielding to our own sin and selfishness clogs our hearts and hinders our ability to love. Accepting and following Christ gives us life and enables us to love others and bring glory to God.

So, why do we need to do the work to process our pain? If you choose to be dictated by your pain, the enemy wins. Period. If you agree with the voice of anxiety, offense, and fear, you open the door to the enemy's bondage. Jesus tells us in John 10:10, *"The thief comes only to steal and kill and destroy. I came that they may have life and have it abundantly."* The thief would love to steal your heart, livelihood, peace, and purpose by subtly making you think you are entitled to unhealthy responses. One of the enemy's most cunning tactics is to lie and steal from you when you are at your weakest - when you are hurt and in pain. By harboring unforgiveness, we open the door to the oppression of the enemy. As we are wise to these schemes, we can overcome them.

When we are fragile, worn down, and vulnerable due to painful circumstances, one of the best things we can do is to lean into others in the body of Christ. When we isolate, we can't overcome. You are not strong enough. You need others. We can't defeat these schemes by ourselves. Who are your people? Where is your local church? Are you planted in the house of the Lord? (Psalm 92:13) You will be strengthened and protected if you stay close to the pack, choose to be vulnerable, and are honest with others in a Bible-teaching church.

God created us to connect for a reason. We were not meant to fight battles alone!

Although it would be nice to not have to fight spiritual battles, we are equipped to fight. If we don't resist our enemy, we will get stuck, derailed, and not experience the abundant life Jesus died for. As Christians, we are enlisted for war and we have everything we need to win. Ephesians 6:11 says, "*Put on the whole armor of God, that you may be able to stand against the schemes of the devil.*" I want to help you armor up, so you don't get beat up, my friend.

What is the enemy really after anyway? He is after your heart. If he can shut down your heart, he can hinder your children, your family, your sphere of influence, and those you are called to love. The devil is after your potential and purpose. He is after your godly family lineage. He is after the glory of the Father in your life. The enemy would love to lock you up, isolate you, and make you ineffective due to pain. You don't have to let him.

You can release, process, receive God's love, and take new territory. You can be free to love those you are called to love. There are people depending on your heart to *FLOW*. As you let God love you and renew your mind in His Word, you can be an agent of consistent love to others. As you receive His love, you are able to give His love and expand the kingdom of God.

Take heart! Jesus tells us in John 16:33, "*In this world you will have tribulation. But take heart; I have overcome the world.*" If Jesus lives inside you, you overcome the challenges of this world too. Don't let the enemy play you.

You can become wise to his schemes. Stay connected to the Source of love: Jesus. Stay connected to others in the Body of Christ.

Stay pure, open, and free, so you can run your race and fulfill your purpose. This world needs your gifts, your calling, and your presence for those you are called to reach. Your life does matter and other people are depending on you keeping your heart alive!

You were created to FLOW:

F - Free

L - to Love

O - Others

W - Well

What if every Christian maintained a vibrant heart and fulfilled his or her distinct purpose? What would the world look like?

_____

_____

_____

_____

_____

_____

_____

_____

_____

_____

_____

_____

_____

_____

Chapter 12

The FLOWing Body of Christ

"The Body of Christ is a multicultural citizenry of an otherworldly kingdom."

David Platt

Just imagine: Christians engaged in their unique purposes, *FLOW*ing in love, and expanding God's Kingdom on the earth. Men and women rising up and shining in the world. Families fueled by love and forgiveness. People saying "Yes" to God's call in their spheres of influence, in their churches, and in the marketplace. Imagine gifts given to each of us from heaven being utilized to strengthen the mandate and Kingdom of Jesus.

When someone faces a trial, instead of isolating, he or she can draw close to others to help in their battle. Wounded and worn-down people can lean on God and each other to reject anxiety, depression, offense, and fear. Imagine the children of God clinging to faith and drawing from the love and faith of those around them. When one is weak, others lift them up.

Husbands and wives can learn how to communicate effectively and demonstrate love to each other and their children. Although imperfect people, they can strive to walk in humility while showing preference to one another in love. What if they speak words of life over one another and refuse to bow to gossip, slander, and hardness of heart? Imagine when someone offends another, we are aware of the bait, and we refuse to take it.

- *What if the Church were wise to the enemy's schemes?*

- *What would it look like if we extended the love we have received?*

- *What would it look like if the Body of Christ was truly FLOWing?*

The Church, the Bride of Christ, would be an unstoppable, radiant force on the earth! We would take our rightful place of authority and dominion and shine as we glorify God and defeat darkness. We can go back to that place of dominion and authority we saw in the garden because Jesus has trampled over death and sin.

We get to choose whether we bow to temptation and take that bite every day. We get to choose whether we walk in the flesh or the Spirit.

I want to encourage you to "get in the game" of God's Kingdom work. Discover the design and spiritual gifts God gave you so you can represent the Kingdom of God in a dark world.

Embrace being planted in a local church with imperfect people. Psalm 92:13 (NKJV) says, "*Those who are planted in the house of the Lord shall flourish in the courts of our God.*" Send your roots deep. We need each other to flourish and *FLOW!*

As you leave these pages, may you solidify the skill of Proverbs 4:23, "*Keep your heart with all vigilance, for from it flow the springs of life.*" My hope and prayer is that you understand a little deeper how necessary the principle and practice of Proverbs 4:23 is. Your heart, health, and destiny depend on it. May you be aware of the enemy's schemes to find an open door in your life through heart pain and may you be wise to shut that door.

I pray the *FLOW* process from King David in Psalm 139 is ingrained into who you are and you make it part of your life-when disappointments hit. I still go through the process when life tries to derail me. As I am wrapping up this book, a new life-change and severe betrayal and disappointment crossed our lives. Sometimes we are tested again and again on the messages we are asked to share with the world. I had to go back to the previous words I had written in this book to remind me what to do and how to process the pain when I was caught up in my emotions.

May you become a pro on how to FILTER your THOUGHTS and EMOTIONS, letting God LOVE you, ORDERING YOUR THOUGHTS, and WILLINGLY REPENTING areas of sin.

I pray you have experienced an opening and *FLOW*ing of your heart through the processing pages of this book.

I hope you found some areas to sweep out that you didn't even know were there. If you were off course, I pray you have been remapped so you can continue running your race and finish strong. May you know how to quickly recognize when an accusation, lie, or sin tries to seep deep into your heart when life happens. Stay in your lane and run the race that is set before you.

If I can leave you with one final thought it would be this one from Hebrews 12:1 (NLT), "*Therefore, since we are surrounded by such a huge crowd of witnesses to the life of faith, let us strip off every weight that slows us down, especially the sin that so easily trips us up. And let us run with endurance the race God has set before us.*" Let's strip off the weights, run our race, and *FLOW* fully in our hearts. May you embrace everything God has for you. I am here cheering you on!

Acknowledgements

One morning, I awoke with a download from the Holy Spirit about this book concept. Getting from concept to completion is a feat. Two weeks and four chapters in, my husband had a serious bike accident, which shifted my focus to caring for him. Over three years later, due to other delays, *"FLOW: Keeping Your Heart Alive When Life Hurts"* is being released.

Throughout this project, no one has believed in it - or me - more than my husband, Jon. He has supported, prayed, and encouraged me to continue on when the warfare came. His belief in this message and in God's assignment for me has given me the courage I needed to finish.

Josiah and Joshua, our sons, have supported me in this writing process as well with insight, shoulder rubs, and coffee refills. I hope I have modeled to them what perseverance looks like when God calls.

I want to thank the brave ladies who shared their testimonies. Although their names were changed, they chose to share intimate details of their lives to help you, the reader. Each story came across my path as I was about to start writing each topic. Surely, God put this book together and sent the stories to me one by one, exactly when it was time to write them. I am so proud of these women.

I am thankful for the editors who believed in me, used their expertise, and put in the extra work to help me push this project forward. Thank you Stephanie, Sarah, and Jon.

Writing is lonely work. Thank you to my friends and family who cheered me on, understanding the sacrifices made and moments missed to be able to complete this assignment.

Most importantly, I thank the Holy Spirit for revelation and precisely crafting each word with me. It has been a joy to partner with Him!

About the Author

Joy Scott is an author and speaker with a passion for helping people find healing, freedom, and purpose. In 2015, she self-published her debut book, "*Joseph's Joy: Living with Unstoppable Hope*," which shared her fierce battle for the life of her firstborn son.

Driven by her own journey through pain and hope, Joy, and her husband, Jon, founded Joseph's Joy, a 501(c)(3) nonprofit that raised tens of thousands of dollars to support families facing the high costs of pediatric medical crises. She also served on the board of the Louisiana chapter of Basket of Hope, a national organization that brings encouragement to children with life-threatening illnesses and their families.

Joy's desire is to help others discover their God-given freedom and purpose, and then encourage them to take concrete steps toward their calling. Her authentic and engaging style makes her a sought-after speaker for both faith-based and professional events. She has delivered keynote messages at over 30 conferences, including Women Mean Business and many other women's events.

Professionally, Joy has served as Marketing Director for Aveda Institutes, overseeing campaigns for 11 cosmetology schools across the Southeast. She has also taught in both public schools and classically homeschooled her two sons. Joy holds an education degree from Southeastern Louisiana University and a Master's Certification from the University of New Orleans.

Though her professional accomplishments are many, she treasures her role as a wife and mother above all. Her husband often refers to her as a modern-day Proverbs 31 woman, and Joy sees the richness of life reflected in meaningful, connected relationships at home.

Whether through speaking, writing, or mentoring, Joy's life message remains clear: no pain is too deep, no past too broken for God to redeem. She lives in the greater New Orleans area with her husband and sons.

You can follow Joy at:

JoyScott.me

facebook.com/joyscott

instagram.com/joy_scott_

youtube.com/@joy_scott

To book Joy for a speaking event, visit JoyScott.me.

Group Discussion Questions

Group 1: Chapters 1-4

Read and work through chapters 1-4 before your group meeting. Choose the questions to best fit your group and timeframe.

Chapter 1 discusses how painful experiences can lead to either "shriveling" or "flowing" in the heart.

What does it mean to "keep your heart" with vigilance as Proverbs 4:23 suggests? How can we actively guard our hearts to maintain emotional and spiritual health?

Chapter 2 has the metaphor of a "kinked hose" to describe how trauma and pain can block the flow of our hearts. In what ways have you noticed your own heart or emotions being "kinked" or blocked?

Chapter 3 opens with statistics on trauma and abuse. How does understanding the widespread nature of trauma impact the way you view your own experiences or those of others?

How does the biblical explanation of choice and free will in the Garden of Eden help you understand the presence of sin, trauma, and suffering in the world?

Joy shares how trauma produces physiological changes in the brain and body. How does knowing this affect your perspective on people who may "overreact" or have unexpected emotional responses?

How can a supportive community or safe relationships serve as a protective factor against trauma? Have you experienced or witnessed this kind of support in your life?

Chapter 4 explains the F.L.O.W. process. Which part of the F.L.O.W. process (Filter Your Thoughts and Emotions, Let God Love You, Order Your Thoughts, and Willingly Repent) feels most natural to you, and which feels the most difficult? Why do you think that is?

Willing repentance is framed not as excusing what happened to us, but as releasing our grip on bitterness, blame, and control. What's one area where you need to stop playing "judge" and let God take over?

Looking back at the full *FLOW* process, what has the Holy Spirit revealed to you about your heart's current state? Where do you sense God inviting you to restore *FLOW* today?

Group 2: Chapter 5

Read and work through Chapter 5 before your group meeting. Choose the questions to best fit your group and timeframe.

Rejection often disguises itself behind performance, perfectionism, or people-pleasing. In what ways have you tried to cover or compensate for feelings of rejection in your own life?

Joy writes, "I felt that if people could see me up close, they would know and run away." Can you relate to this fear of being truly seen? What would it look like to let yourself be fully known and loved anyway?

Kelli's story illustrates how buried trauma and rejection can resurface years later. Are there past wounds in your own life that the Holy Spirit might be bringing to the surface now—not to shame you, but to heal you?

Rejection can whisper lies like "you're unworthy," "you're unwanted," or "you're not enough." What lie of rejection has tried to attach itself to your identity? What truth from God's Word can replace that lie?

The chapter says, "Rejection is not your identity." What steps can you take to shift from identifying with rejection to embracing your identity as God's beloved child?

In what ways have you unintentionally agreed with the spirit of rejection (e.g., self-rejection, isolation, harsh self-talk)? What might it look like to break that agreement and step into agreement with God's voice instead?

When we are rejected, we often respond with fight, flight, freeze, or fawn. Which of these reactions shows up most in your life—and what does it look like to surrender that pattern to God?

What is your next step in restoring *FLOW* to the areas of your heart affected by rejection? (Filtering your thoughts, letting God love you, ordering your thoughts and willingly repenting)

Group 3: Chapter 6

Read and work through Chapter 6 before your group meeting. Choose the questions to best fit your group and timeframe.

In this chapter Ava showed up to celebrate others even in the middle of her pain. Have you ever had to show up for someone else while carrying your own disappointment? How did that feel—and what did it reveal about your heart or faith?

Ava was asked a difficult but powerful question: "Would God be enough for her to worship without a child?" What is your version of that question? What are you tempted to believe you "must have" to keep trusting or worshiping God?

The story of Hannah shows us that waiting and disappointment do not mean God is absent. How has a season of delay impacted your relationship with God—did it create distance, or did it deepen your dependence on Him?

Disappointment often whispers lies like "God is withholding from me" or "There must be something wrong with me." What lie has disappointment tried to make you believe about yourself or about God?

Ava's journey reminds us that God may be doing something far greater than we can see. Can you look back at a past disappointment and now see a greater purpose God was working through? How might that perspective encourage you in your current season?

In what ways has disappointment tempted you to withdraw from community, joy, or even God? What would it take to move from isolation to engagement again?

Psalm 34:18 says, "The Lord is close to the brokenhearted." How have you personally experienced or struggled to experience God's closeness in your broken places?

Disappointment invites us to either "bail on God or believe in God." What would it mean for you, today, to choose belief over bitterness in one specific area of your life?

Hannah gave back her miracle to God in worship. If God granted your deepest desire, how would you steward it for His glory?

Group 4: Chapter 7

Read and work through Chapter 7 before your group meeting. Choose the questions to best fit your group and timeframe.

How does Exodus 14:14 ("The Lord himself will fight for you. Just stay calm.") speak into your current or past struggles with injustice?

Cara faced deep betrayal, grief, and injustice. What part of her story resonated with you the most—and why?

Have you ever faced a moment where forgiveness felt like an impossible decision, yet God asked you to release control?

In what ways does Cara's transformation from pain to purpose inspire or challenge you? Can you identify a place in your life where God might be inviting you to shift from bitterness to breakthrough?

What stood out to you in the story of Hagar (Genesis 16)? How do you relate to Hagar's feelings of abandonment, powerlessness, or being unseen?

Genesis 16:13 says, "You are the God who sees me." In what ways does knowing God sees you change the way you process your pain or injustices?

What emotions or thoughts rise up when you reflect on your own experiences of injustice? How have those thoughts shaped how you see yourself, others, or even God?

God asks us to forgive even when it feels unjust. What barriers do you experience in forgiving someone who has hurt you or someone you love? What would it look like to begin releasing that today?

Psalm 139 paints a picture of a deeply personal, loving Creator. How can reflecting on your unique creation and God's constant presence help you reframe painful experiences in your life?

The Bible is clear that injustice is not overlooked by God (Proverbs 17:15, Romans 12:19). What helps you trust God to deal with injustice in His time and His way?

Group 5: Chapter 8

Read and work through Chapter 8 before your group meeting. Choose the questions to best fit your group and timeframe.

Ellen asked herself whether she would stay "under the covers" or reimagine a life after loss. What "covers" have you been tempted to stay under in your grief, and what would it mean for you to reimagine a future with God's help?

"Sometimes you have to let go of the picture of what you thought it would be like." What picture or dream have you had to release due to loss? How has God met you—or how do you hope He will—in the "story you are actually living"?

Ellen had to choose whether pain would defeat her or propel her into purpose. Where are you right now on that path—are you more defined by your pain, or are you beginning to glimpse purpose rising from it?

Ruth lost everything and still chose to follow Naomi and Naomi's God. What does Ruth's courage and loyalty teach you about trust in the midst of grief and the unknown?

The Bible says Ruth "found favor" even in her sorrow (Ruth 2:13). Have you been able to see moments of God's favor or tenderness—even in your grieving season? If not yet, what would it take to open your heart to that possibility?

Ellen realized her emotions were real, but God's Word was the truth she would cling to. What truth from Scripture do you need to believe right now that feels hard to accept emotionally?

Loss can challenge what we believe about ourselves and about God. What lie has grief tempted you to believe? What truth from God's Word can replace it?

Romans 5 reminds us that "hope does not disappoint." Where in your life do you need to fight to believe that hope is still possible?

Ellen's grief became a platform to encourage and walk with others. What pain or experience might God be asking you to one day use to minister hope to someone else?

Group 6: Chapter 9

Read and work through Chapter 9 before your group meeting. Choose the questions to best fit your group and timeframe.

Why do you think Maria didn't recognize her resentment earlier, even though she was deeply frustrated? What does this reveal about how resentment can quietly build in our lives?

Have you ever, like Maria or Joy, felt justified in holding onto resentment? What did that do to your relationships, your communication, or your spiritual health?

The chapter discusses how resentment can stem from feeling misunderstood or unacknowledged. Can you identify a time when you felt this way? How did you respond, and how would you respond differently now?

Cain's story in Genesis 4 highlights unchecked resentment leading to destruction. What are some warning signs in your own life that resentment may be brewing?

How do people-pleasing tendencies contribute to unspoken resentment, as seen in Maria's story? Where might you be minimizing your feelings to avoid conflict?

Joy mentions that resentment often grows when we over-give or sacrifice without feeling seen or validated. In what areas of your life might this be true? What conversations need to happen?

What role does healthy, honest communication play in preventing or resolving resentment in relationships? How have you seen this work (or fail) in your own marriage, family, or friendships?

What does it look like practically to "make an exchange" with God—trading resentment for grace, hurt for healing? Have you ever done this? What was the outcome?

The chapter ends with a call to repentance, not just for what was done to us, but for how we respond. Is there any area where the Holy Spirit is inviting you to repent, forgive, or communicate more openly today?

Group 7: Chapter 10

Read and work through Chapter 10 before your group meets. Choose the questions to best fit your group and timeframe.

Have you ever had to choose between trusting God and clinging to your preferred outcome?

What does obedience look like in your current season, even when it's painful or unclear?

Fear and anxiety affected Lauren's ability to express her needs. Have you ever suppressed your emotions out of fear of being a burden? What was the result?

Lauren said, "It was never about staying or leaving, but guarding her heart." What does it mean to guard your heart (Proverbs 4:23) in the midst of betrayal and hardship?

Abigail intervened to protect her household from the fallout of her husband's foolishness. What does it take to act in wisdom and humility under pressure, especially when someone else's actions endanger your peace?

Lauren contended for her heart and chose not to let bitterness take root. What practices help you keep your heart soft and surrendered when you're tempted to become bitter?

Both Abigail and Lauren honored God by showing love to those who didn't deserve it. Can you recall a time when God asked you to love someone who had deeply hurt you? How did you choose to respond?

How have you seen spiritual warfare show up in your relationships, and how have you fought through it?

Group 8: Chapters 11-12

Read and work through Chapters 11-12 before your group meeting. Choose the questions that best fit your group and timeframe.

Chapter 11 opens by highlighting how love has become a casual word in our culture. In your experience, what makes someone truly feel loved? How does that differ from simply saying "I love you"?

Isolation is one of the enemy's tactics. Are you currently planted in a church community or circle of believers that strengthens your faith? If not, what's holding you back?

"If the enemy can shut down your heart, he can hinder your children, your family, your sphere of influence." How have you seen spiritual warfare affect your purpose, family, or relationships? What needs to be protected right now?

You were created to *FLOW*: Free to Love Others Well. What would change in your life if you fully lived out this identity?

What does it mean for the Body of Christ to "*FLOW*" together, and what role do you personally play in that flow?

How are you using your gifts, influence, or experiences to strengthen the Church and expand the Kingdom?

What schemes of the enemy do you think are most common or dangerous to the modern Church? How can we remain vigilant and protect our hearts from these traps (see Proverbs 4:23)?

How does being "planted" in a local church affect your spiritual growth and fruitfulness? What might be keeping you (or others) from fully committing to a spiritual community?

What has been most impactful to you from this book and time together? How have you healed?

Endnotes

1   National Coalition Against Violence, http://urlncadv.org, accessed 27, July, 2025

2   Black, M.C., Basile, K.C., Breiding, M.J., Smith, S.G., Walters, M.L., Merrick, M.T., Chen, J., & Stevens, M.R. (2011). The National Intimate Partner and Sexual Violence Survey (NISVS): 2010 Summary Report. Atlanta, GA: National Center for Injury Prevention and Control, Centers for Disease Control and Prevention.

3   Van der Kolk, Bessel A., The Body Keeps the Score: Brain, Mind, and Body in the Healing of Trauma, New York: Viking, 2014, 150-151

4   Van der Kolk, Bessel A. The Body Keeps the Score: Brain, Mind, and Body in the Healing of Trauma. Viking, 2014, 21

5   Van der Kolk, Bessell A.,The Body Keeps the Score: Brain, Mind, and Body in the Healing of Trauma, Viking, 2014, Chapter 13

6   Van der Kolk, Bessel A., The Body Keeps the Score: Brain, Mind, and Body in the Healing of Trauma, Viking, 2014, ch. 5

7   Gossett Jr., Louis. An Actor and a Gentleman. Wiley, 2010, p. 222

8   Spurgeon, Charles H. Morning and Evening. Edited by Alistair Begg, Crossway, 2003. Evening Devotion for March 27.

9   David Platt, Counter Culture: Following Christ in an Anti-Christian Age (Carol Stream, IL: Tyndale House Publishers, 2015), 219.

www.ingramcontent.com/pod-product-compliance
Lightning Source LLC
Chambersburg PA
CBHW071219090426
42736CB00014B/2902